Tana Ramsay
home made

Tana Ramsay
home made

Good, honest food made easy

HarperCollins*Publishers*

To Meg, Jack, Holly and Tilly – my four babes x

COOK'S NOTES

Butter: The type of butter is specified where it is critical.

Citrus fruit: If you're using the zest of oranges and lemons, buy unwaxed fruit. If you can't find this, wash the fruit in hot water before use.

Eggs: These are medium size unless specified otherwise. I use free-range eggs.

Poultry: I buy free-range wherever possible.

Salt and pepper: Generally I use sea salt flakes and freshly ground black pepper; sometimes white pepper is more appropriate and a finer or coarser grade of salt is required, and the recipe will tell you this.

Spoon measures: All spoon measures are level unless otherwise stated.

HarperCollins*Publishers*
77–85 Fulham Palace Road,
Hammersmith, London W6 8JB
www.harpercollins.co.uk

First published by HarperCollins*Publishers* 2008. This edition 2010

10 9 8 7 6 5 4 3 2 1

© Tana Ramsay 2008

Photographs © Jill Mead
Food styling: Karen Taylor
Styling: Penny Markham
Home economist: Alexandra Howard

Tana Ramsay asserts the moral right to be identified as the author of this work

Moiré pattern on chapter openers, wooden spoon p.i © Getty Images
Patterned silk on chapter introductions © The Art Archive/Gianni Dagli Orti

A catalogue record of this book is available from the British Library

ISBN 978-0-00-727609-7

Printed and bound in Italy by L.E.G.O. SpA

Contents

Introduction

Home has always been the most important place in my life – from my earliest childhood memories when home was the farm I lived on with my parents, brothers and sister, right up to today when home is where Gordon, the kids and I retreat to from the chaos of our busy lives. Even the word 'home' conjures up so many emotions for me – happiness, love, security; it's my haven from the world outside.

When I was growing up in the country, life seemed much simpler than it does today. On non-school days my brothers, sister and I would leave the house early in the morning and run around the fields, making camps amongst the hay bales and only returning home when we were hungry. My children don't have such freedom to roam in the modern city, but, just as we were, they are out at school and other activities from early in the morning and really active from dawn to dusk. And as they get older, life seems to get even busier.

Weekdays are usually pretty chaotic, and after all the rushing around, the place we all long to be is home, where we can have time out and find some sense of peace (as much as you can with four boisterous children bouncing around the house!). Home is the place where my family and I can switch off and just be. As a family of two working parents and four busy schoolchildren, coming home gives us the opportunity to be together, to take a break from the madness and pause long enough to catch up on everything that's going on.

Once through the door, the coats and bags are put away and we all switch from working mode into a more relaxed atmosphere. We usually end up in the kitchen and talk about our days and all the things that made it good or bad – doing well at sport or lessons, something nice that someone said, not making the school team or play, or the friendship fall-outs and fights. All these things can be poured out within the comfort and security of our home, where we all know that none of us will judge the other, but just listen. This is home. This is where, for us, real life happens.

Even before I had my children, creating a sense of home was important to me; just as now it is a place for us to talk with the children, so it was for Gordon and me before they arrived on the scene. When we first met he was working late every night and I was working all day and studying to be a Montessori teacher in the evenings, but even then we would have a cup of tea in the small hours when he got home so that we could spend time together (something we still do now). Like any other mother, I want the best for our children; I want them to be happy and healthy and remember their childhood as fondly as I do mine. Even though my childhood in the country was very different to their urban lifestyle, the one thing that remains the same is having that sense of security and peace. And that's what I believe a home is all about.

My mother is my inspiration for how to run a home; no matter how busy she was, she would always have time for us and would make sure that we had everything we needed. My mother puts me to shame: not only did she manage the farm, the home and cook all our food from scratch, but she also still made sure that she always had her lipstick on! When my brothers and sister and I would come home from school or play, tired from our exertions and having worked up an appetite, there would always be a meal ready and waiting for us, and I can even remember a time when everything on the table – from the butter to the wine – was made by her.

Like my mother, I have this idea that there are some things that only I can do for my children, and if you ask my friends and family about this they'll tell you that I like to do everything myself. Unlike my mother, I have no desire to make my own butter, bread, or even wine, but I do feel passionately about providing the family with healthy, nutritious and home-cooked food. Before I had children, good soulful home-cooked food was something that I reminisced about; certain smells and dishes have always reminded me of places and people in my life and spark happy memories of growing up with my family and of my mother's amazing cooking, but now I see it as an essential part of creating a sense of home for my own family.

Because my weekdays are usually spent juggling work and ferrying the children between school and post-school activities, I find that the best way of ensuring these meals are on the table every night is to plan them in advance. Getting ahead a few days at a time means that I always know what I'm going to be cooking and don't have to think about it as the children spill through the door, tired, hungry and expectantly sniffing for the comforting smells from the kitchen that will reassure them their dinner is on its way. Sometimes this planning might only go as far as knowing that I'm going to cook chicken one night and fish or pasta another, and then it's a case of raiding the cupboard or the fridge and perhaps using up what's in there to go with it. But that's often enough to make life easier, and I love being able to pull out various ingredients to produce something quick and delicious from a few odds and ends. Of course, I've cooked all the recipes in this book at some time or another, but if I'm honest, the majority were created just by experimenting with what ingredients I had at the time.

So that's why this new collection of recipes is based around my favourite core ingredients: chicken and duck, beef, fish and seafood, lamb, pork, vegetables, potatoes, fruit and chocolate, and also essential dishes such as soups, pizza and pasta. My aim is to give you inspiration for those times when you stand staring into the fridge wondering what to do with the chicken thighs, pork, or salmon fillet that you want to cook tonight, and to give you a few new options for easy ways to pep up essential basic ingredients with just a few extra ones. Good honest home cooking doesn't need to be complicated; even putting the simplest meal on the table should warm the heart and restore the soul, just because it gives you the opportunity to sit down together as a family.

My attitude to cooking – and to family life in general – is quite relaxed and not precious, and I suppose I'm more of a 'chuck it all in the pan' kind of cook. This is probably because, on busy weeknights when the family are all returning home at different hours, I don't have time to mess around with complicated dishes and getting everything just so. If I do follow a recipe, I use it as the skeleton of a dish, and I'll happily substitute one vegetable for another that I have in the fridge that needs using up, for instance, or use something that looked particularly appealing when I was out shopping. So when following any recipe, mine included, my advice would be to not get hung up on quantities – if there are three mushrooms left in the bag more than the recipe calls for, chuck them in too, or if the recipe demands two celery sticks and you have only one, don't rush down to the supermarket to buy it. Getting a meal on the table for the family after a long day at work or doing other things can be stressful enough, so why make it more complicated than it needs to be?

So if, like me, you think about your meals in advance and like to have meat or chicken a couple of times a week, or pasta once, or keep desserts only for the weekend, then I hope this book will help you to make a few decisions on what you're going to cook. The chapters here are divided up by the ingredients I cook with most at home and reflect how I plan the meals for my lot. Whether you're cooking a revitalizing supper for a horde of hungry schoolchildren, a lovely, homely meal for the frazzled family winding down on a Friday night, a lazy weekend lunch for friends and extended family, or a cosy meal à deux after the kids have gone to bed, I hope you can find something here that suits your needs, keeps your family happy at the end of a day, and that the look on their faces as they tuck in will remind you just how good home cooking can be.

Simply
SOUPS

Where would we be without soups? I love them for their sheer all-roundness; they're possibly the ultimate comfort food – winter or summer. A hearty warming bowl of soup is always gratefully received after a cold wet couple of hours running around a sports pitch (or, for us, standing on the sidelines!), or after an energetic swimming lesson that leaves the children starving and in need of heat and sustenance. Equally, a refreshing, chilled gazpacho on a hot summer's day can perfectly bridge the gap between the food and fluids you need to keep going – satisfying a light appetite and quenching your thirst.

My kids have eaten soup from an early age because it was always something they could tackle by themselves – which meant one less battle with toddlers trying to exert their independence! Even now soup is one of their favourite meals for supper or lunch, especially

eaten from a mug, which they love to wrap
their fingers around on a cold day, with warm
good bread to dunk in the soup as they eat.
Even the heartiest soup makes a great light
supper late at night when you don't want
anything too heavy before you go to sleep.

Some of these recipes need an hour or so
to cook through, which makes them ideal
evening meals that can be part- or fully-
prepared earlier in the day. If I'm at home and
not rushing out somewhere, I'll often prepare
food in the morning so that when everyone
returns home dinner is either bubbling away
on the stove, or can be reheated quickly to
feed them instantly. Most of these soups,
especially the gazpacho, can also even benefit
from being prepared the night before – either
while the children are eating their dinner or
made, with a glass of wine in your hand, once
they've gone to bed...

Comforting chicken soup

Spicy fish soup

Cullen skink

Pearl barley, Savoy cabbage and
chorizo soup

Sweetcorn and coconut soup

Spicy lentil and cannellini bean soup

Green minestrone soup

Gazpacho

Mushroom soup with truffle oil
and chives

Sweet potato and carrot soup with a
chilli oil sprinkling

Comforting chicken soup

A perfect pick-me-up.

1 chicken weighing about
   1.25kg/2³/₄lb
1 stick of celery, sliced
1 carrot, peeled and halved
2 leeks, white parts only,
   cleaned, trimmed and chopped
2 medium onions, peeled
   and chopped
1 bay leaf
6 peppercorns
1 sprig of tarragon
50g/2oz butter
2 tbsp plain flour
100ml/3¹/₂fl oz whipping
   cream
1 tbsp dry sherry
salt
1 small bunch of chives,
   finely sliced, to garnish

Serves: 4-6
Prep time: 30 minutes
Cooking time: 1 hour
50 minutes plus cooling

1 Choose a saucepan, with a lid, that fits the chicken and allows a little room for other vegetables. Put the chicken into the centre of the pot and surround with the celery, carrot and half the leeks and onions. Throw in the bay leaf, peppercorns, tarragon and a generous pinch of salt and pour over enough water almost to cover the bird, leaving the top of the breast clear. It will poach in the steam. Put on the hob and bring to the boil, then reduce the heat to a slow simmer. Put on the lid and cook very gently for 1¹/₂ hours.

2 When the time is up, remove from the heat and allow to cool for as long as it takes to remove the chicken safely. Put the chicken to one side.

3 Pour the cooking liquor through a fine sieve into a clean pan and discard all the vegetables and seasonings. Boil the liquor until reduced to about 1 litre/1¹/₂ pints.

4 Meanwhile, in a clean pan, melt the butter on a medium heat and add the remaining chopped onion and leek. Fry until soft, but not coloured. Add the flour and stir well to make a smooth paste around the vegetables. Fry for a couple of minutes, then gradually stir in the reduced cooking liquor. Increase the heat and bring to the boil, stirring all the time. Reduce the heat and simmer for 10 minutes. Remove from the heat and allow to cool slightly, then liquidize in batches.

5 Return the liquidized mixture to the saucepan and bring back to a simmer. Add the cream and sherry.

6 Using your hands, remove the breast meat from the chicken carcass, discarding the skin. Shred the meat into very small pieces and add to the soup. Season with salt to taste and serve in warm bowls, sprinkled with the chives.

When we've had a really full day, or we've battled through bad weather and traffic to get home, or if someone is feeling ill or down, nothing beats a simple supper to revive the spirits.

We all have foods we crave when we're not feeling 100 per cent; Megan loves my chicken soup, and Holly egg and soldiers, while Jack and Matilda are comforted by anything on toast. In our family, soups are right up there on the list of comfort foods, along with juicy steak sandwiches, fluffy mash, deliciously fresh and zingy salmon steaks, or a perfectly cooked roast. Desserts are a weekend thing for us, and none of us crave them during the week, so simple, savoury food is usually enough to lift the mood and cast aside the cares of the day.

I'm a great believer in the power of food to heal and soothe; and by this I don't mean reaching for the chocolate as soon as you get through the door to make yourself feel better. Normally I find that listening to my body and having just a little of what I crave works wonders.

Spicy fish soup

This is perfect for serving as a meal for the entire family. Add Tabasco to taste for those who prefer a chilli kick – my grandfather and son always used to fight over who could handle the most Tabasco!

3 tbsp olive oil
4 large onions, peeled and
    roughly chopped
4 garlic cloves, peeled and
    finely chopped
2 red chillies, deseeded and
    finely chopped
3 each red and green peppers,
    deseeded and chopped
400g tin of chopped tomatoes
1.5 litres/2$^{1}/_{2}$ pints good-
    quality fish stock
2 tsp fresh or dried marjoram
$^{1}/_{2}$–1 tsp cayenne pepper
700g/1$^{1}/_{2}$lb fresh cod or
    pollack, skinned and cut into
    4cm/1$^{1}/_{2}$ inch chunks
100g/3$^{1}/_{2}$oz peeled raw
    prawns
1 tbsp chopped fresh
    flat-leaf parsley
salt and black pepper
Tabasco sauce to serve

1 Choose a large saucepan with a lid. Heat the oil in the pan on a low-medium heat and add the onions along with the garlic and chillies. Cover and cook for 8–10 minutes, until softened. Add the red and green peppers and sweat until softened slightly.

2 Pour the contents of the pan into a food processor along with the tomatoes and blend until smooth.

3 Return the mixture to the saucepan and add the stock, marjoram and cayenne pepper. Bring to the boil, then reduce the heat and simmer for about 10 minutes. Add salt to taste, then stir in the fish and prawns and cook gently for no more than 10 minutes – be careful not to overcook.

4 Add the parsley and serve in warm bowls. The Tabasco and a grinding of black pepper should be added to taste once the soup is served.

Serves: 6–8
Prep time: 30 minutes
Cooking time: 30 minutes

WHY NOT TRY...

If cooking for a dinner party, try roasting and skinning the peppers before adding to the soup.

Cullen skink

Good-quality smoked haddock fillet is essential to this recipe as its flavour is crucial to the success of the finished soup. I prefer to use Charlotte potatoes as they keep their colour and shape.

60g/2^{1}/$_{2}$oz butter
2 medium onions, peeled and
   finely chopped
1kg/2^{1}/$_{4}$lb Charlotte potatoes,
   peeled and diced into
   1cm/^{1}/$_{2}$ inch cubes
800ml/1 pint 7fl oz full-fat milk
500g/1lb 2oz undyed smoked
   haddock fillet
50ml/2fl oz whipping cream
black pepper and perhaps a
   little salt
chopped chives to garnish

Serves: 4-6
Prep time: 20 minutes
Cooking time: 30 minutes
plus 10 minutes standing

1 Choose a large saucepan with a tight-fitting lid. Melt the butter in the pan on a low-medium heat, add the onions and fry for 5 minutes, until softening. Add the potatoes and continue to fry for another 5 minutes or so until they are just beginning to soften. Add the milk and bring to the boil, then reduce the heat and simmer for 5 minutes.

2 Lay the haddock on top of the potatoes and milk, folding the thin end of the tail underneath, if necessary, so it fits in the pan. Cover with the lid and reduce the heat to a minimum so that it is barely simmering. Cook for 10 minutes. Remove from the heat. Keep the lid on and leave for a further 10 minutes, until the haddock is just cooked.

3 Remove the haddock from the pan, place on a plate and leave until cool enough to handle. Flake the flesh, discarding the skin and any bones. Return the fish to the pan, season with pepper and a little salt if necessary, and stir gently to combine. Add the cream and slowly bring back to the boil.

4 Serve in warm bowls, garnished with chives and ground black pepper, and accompanied by plenty of crusty brown bread.

Pearl barley, Savoy cabbage and chorizo soup

This hearty soup will chase away damp, cold days, especially if you make it with a spicy chorizo sausage. It goes down especially well with my lot after football and swimming lessons when they always come home ravenously hungry.

3 tbsp extra virgin olive oil
2 red onions, peeled and finely chopped
2 garlic cloves, peeled and finely chopped
2 sprigs of thyme
250g/9oz chorizo sausages, skinned and chopped into bite-sized pieces
$1/2$ Savoy cabbage, shredded
100g/$3^1/_2$oz pearl barley
squeeze of lemon juice
1 handful of chopped fresh parsley, chopped
salt and black pepper

1 Heat the oil in a large saucepan on a low-medium heat. Add the onions, garlic and thyme and cook gently for about 5 minutes, until softened but not coloured. Add the sausages and fry for 4–5 minutes until the oil begins to run. Meanwhile, put on the kettle to boil.

2 Add the cabbage and pearl barley to the sausages and pour in enough boiling water to cover everything generously. Bring to bubbling, then reduce the heat and cook gently for 50–60 minutes, until the barley is tender; top up with more hot water if the mixture gets too dry.

3 Add a squeeze of lemon juice and season with salt and pepper to taste. Toss in the parsley, stir through and serve in warm bowls with lots of crusty bread with butter.

Serves: 4
Prep time: 20 minutes
Cooking time: about 1 hour

Spicy lentil and cannellini bean soup

This is a fantastic winter soup, perfect for popping in a flask and taking on a bracing walk.

2 rashers of unsmoked streaky
  bacon
1 tbsp olive oil
1 medium onion, peeled and
  diced
2 carrots, peeled and sliced
1 garlic clove, peeled and sliced
1 tsp garam masala
$^1/_4$ tsp chilli flakes
150g/5oz red lentils
400g tin of chopped tomatoes
400g tin of cannellini beans,
  drained through a sieve and
  then rinsed
1 tbsp tomato purée
1 litre/1$^3/_4$ pints hot water
2 good-quality chicken stock
  cubes
$^1/_2$ tsp sugar
zest of 1 lemon
salt and black pepper
4 tbsp plain yoghurt to serve
coriander leaves, roughly
  chopped, to garnish

Serves: 4-6
Prep time: 25 minutes
Cooking time: about 1 hour

1 Choose a large saucepan with a lid. Cut the bacon into short strips. Heat the oil in the pan on a medium heat, add the bacon and fry until lightly coloured. Add the onion and carrots and fry for 8–10 minutes, until softened. Add the garlic, garam masala and chilli flakes and cook for a further minute or so. Stir in the red lentils.

2 Add the tomatoes, cannellini beans, tomato purée and water. Crumble in the stock cubes and stir well. Increase the heat and bring to the boil, stirring all the time so that the lentils do not stick to the bottom of the pan. Reduce the heat to a very gentle simmer and pop the lid on the saucepan. Simmer for 45 minutes, stirring from time to time, until the lentils and carrots are tender.

3 Remove from the heat and allow to cool a bit, then add the sugar and lemon zest and season with salt and pepper to taste. Bring back to the boil and simmer for 2 minutes.

4 Serve in warm bowls. Add a dollop of yoghurt in the middle of each bowl and sprinkle with the coriander.

Green minestrone soup

This is a really hearty minestrone without the predictable tomato offering, which keeps it looking fresh. The slight crunch of chickpeas gives it a little more bite.

2 tbsp olive oil

2 medium onions, peeled and finely chopped

2 garlic cloves, peeled and finely chopped

120g pack of prosciutto (or pancetta), cut into chunks

2 sticks of celery, cut into 5mm/¼ inch slices

400g tin each of cannellini beans and chickpeas, drained through a sieve and then rinsed

3 bay leaves

750ml/1¼ pints chicken stock

125g/4oz dried spaghetti

3 baby courgettes, cut into 5mm/¼ inch slices

100g/3½oz green beans

125g/4oz fine asparagus

1 large handful of spinach, washed

fresh basil, roughly torn

salt and black pepper

freshly grated Parmesan cheese to serve

Serves: 4-6
Prep time: 30 minutes
Cooking time: 25 minutes

1 Heat the oil in a large pan on a low-medium heat, then gently fry the onions, garlic and prosciutto (or pancetta) for 8-10 minutes, until softened. Add the celery along with salt and a good helping of pepper – go easy on the salt as the prosciutto is salty. Add the cannellini beans, chickpeas, bay leaves and stock and bring to the boil. At this point you can leave the base of your soup to simmer for 5 minutes, or leave it to cool and continue later, reheating it before adding the remaining ingredients.

2 You can buy minestrone pasta but it is slightly more old fashioned. Place the spaghetti in the centre of a thin, clean tea towel and roll it up like a cigar/Christmas cracker, nice and tightly. Place the tip of the roll at the edge of the table, push against the table and pull down. This breaks the pasta up beautifully, slightly uneven but perfect for a rustic soup.

3 As soon as you add the pasta and other vegetables to the soup, you need to be careful of your timings so as not to overcook – the soup is so much nicer with slightly crunchy veg and al dente pasta. Add the pasta, courgettes, green beans and asparagus to the soup and simmer for about 8 minutes, until the veg are ready and the pasta al dente. Lastly, add the spinach and cook for 1 minute or so, until wilted. Adjust the seasoning and top with a handful of basil.

4 To serve, ladle into large warm bowls and sprinkle some Parmesan over the top. Alternatively, add a teaspoon of pesto (see page 214) per serving.

Gazpacho

Under no circumstances make this soup at any other time than in high summer, or it will be flavourless and very disappointing. Gazpacho is a very personal soup and everyone who makes it has their own recipe. This is mine, which is very quick and easy to make and is also very healthy.

Ideally, make the soup a day before you need it and keep in the fridge so the flavours can develop. Serve straight from the fridge with 1cm/$^1/_2$ inch slices of French bread brushed with olive oil and baked in the oven at 180°C/350°F/GM4 for 10 minutes.

1 green pepper, deseeded
1 red pepper, deseeded
$^1/_2$ cucumber
3 tbsp tarragon vinegar
  (or white wine vinegar)
3 tbsp good-quality extra
  virgin olive oil
10g pack of fresh tarragon,
  leaves only, finely chopped
400g/14oz ripe tomatoes
1 red onion, peeled
1 mild red chilli, deseeded
1 garlic clove, peeled
750ml/1$^1/_4$ pints good-quality
  tomato juice
salt and black pepper
6 ice cubes to serve

Serves: 6
Prep time: 30 minutes plus chilling, preferably overnight

1 First, reserve one quarter of each green and red pepper and a 2cm/$^3/_4$ inch slice of the cucumber. Put into an airtight container and keep in the fridge until just before serving the soup. When you are ready to make the garnish, finely chop these vegetables and place in a small bowl with 1 tablespoon of the tarragon vinegar and 1 tablespoon of the oil. Stir the chopped tarragon through and set to one side.

2 To make the soup, put the tomatoes, the remaining green and red peppers and cucumber, the onion, chilli and garlic in a food processor and roughly chop. Pour in half the tomato juice and process for a couple of minutes until the vegetables are finely chopped.

3 Add the remaining tarragon vinegar and oil and blitz for a few seconds. Season well with salt and pepper and taste. Pour into a large bowl, stir in the rest of the tomato juice and put in the fridge to cool thoroughly for up to 24 hours. (If you need the soup in a hurry, place in the freezer for 30 minutes instead.)

4 When ready to serve, pour the soup into six bowls and divide the chopped garnish between each bowl. Finally, add an ice cube to each and serve.

Mushroom soup with truffle oil and chives

Whenever I am making this soup I have to remind myself of the finished dish in a pretty white bowl – it's not a beautiful colour while it's cooking, but it tastes delicious, trust me! For a truly indulgent twist, garnish with crumbled Stilton.

3 tbsp olive oil
60g/2^{1}/$_{2}$oz butter
2 medium onions, peeled and roughly chopped
2 garlic cloves, peeled and chopped
900g/2lb flat mushrooms, roughly chopped
200g/7oz button mushrooms, roughly sliced
1 handful of parsley, roughly chopped
300–450ml/10–15fl oz milk (semi- or full-fat)
200g/7oz half-fat crème fraîche (or full-fat, if you prefer), plus 4 tsp crème fraîche to garnish
truffle oil for drizzling
1^{1}/$_{2}$ tbsp roughly chopped chives
salt and black pepper

Serves: 4 generous portions
Prep time: 30 minutes
Cooking time: about 40 minutes

1 Heat the oil and butter in a large frying pan on a low-medium heat, add the onions and garlic and cook for 8–10 minutes, until softened.

2 Increase the heat and add the mushrooms – it will look like a huge amount but they do shrink so much. Throw in the parsley and about 1 teaspoon of salt, then grind in some pepper. Cook, stirring, for a few minutes, until the mushrooms have shrunk enough to fit comfortably in the pan. They will give off some liquid; continue cooking for about 20 minutes, until the liquid has evaporated and the mushrooms are completely tender.

3 Put the mushroom mixture into a food processor along with about 150ml/5fl oz water and blitz – you don't want it completely smooth, but leave it fairly thick.

4 Transfer to a saucepan and add 300ml/10fl oz milk and the crème fraîche. Add more milk if necessary to get the soup to the right consistency. Bring to boiling point and check the seasoning – be very generous with the pepper. As I said before, the soup at this stage does not look appetizing! However, as it heats through, the smell and taste are amazing.

5 Serve the soup in warm bowls, add 1 teaspoon of crème fraîche in the centre of each, drizzle the truffle oil over and sprinkle with chives – delicious.

Sweet potato and carrot soup with a chilli oil sprinkling

I like to serve this soup as a first course, or alongside a sandwich to add a warming element to a quick lunch. It's great for using up stray carrots and sweet potatoes from the fridge drawer! If you are reheating the soup, you may need to add a little more stock to thin it.

2 tsp fresh thyme leaves

6 tbsp chilli oil

2 tbsp olive oil

2 medium onions, peeled and roughly sliced

1 garlic clove, peeled and roughly chopped

750g/1lb 11oz sweet potatoes, peeled and diced

400g/14oz carrots, peeled and sliced

2 knobs of butter

2 Parmesan crusts

1 sprig of rosemary

about 750ml/1¼ pints stock (I use chicken)

salt and black pepper

1 small tub of crème fraîche to serve

Serves: 6
Prep time: 20 minutes
Cooking time: 1 hour

1   Before doing anything, place the thyme leaves in a mortar and pestle and give them a good grinding. Add the chilli oil and leave to infuse while you make the soup.

2   Heat the olive oil in a large pan on a low-medium heat and fry the onions and garlic for 8–10 minutes, until softened. Add the sweet potatoes, carrots, butter, Parmesan crusts and rosemary (still in a whole sprig), season well with salt and pepper and let them sweat down until they start to soften. This tends to happen quicker if you cover the pan – use tin foil tightly sealed around the top of the pan if you don't have a lid – I spend far too much time trying to find lids!

3   Once the vegetables have started to soften (and not before, as we want to intensify the flavour of the vegetables), add the stock and bring to the boil. Cover the pan and simmer for 20–25 minutes until the vegetables are really tender.

4   Once you have reached this stage, remove the Parmesan crusts and the rosemary sprig with a slotted spoon and scrape off any melted softened bits of Parmesan into the vegetables. Tip the soup into a blender and whiz until completely smooth. Return to the pan and check the seasoning.

5   Transfer to a warm serving bowl or bowls and serve with a spoon of crème fraîche in the centre, then drizzle over the thyme-infused chilli oil.

Simply
CHICKEN & DUCK

We all love chicken, especially as individual pies on our plates, or spooned out as a wonderful thick stew from the huge pan bubbling on the stove. On warmer days, or when we're not so hungry, a light stir-fry or simple grilled chicken breast with a fresh green salad always goes down well. A roast chicken is equally simple to prepare and will keep the children at the table for ages, picking away at the bird; and if there's any left over it will do for a soup, a salad, or to fill sandwiches. Don't think of a roast just as a winter dish, either – a roasted chicken can be flavoured with summery citrus flavours and herbs and taste just as delicious with new potatoes and salad as with a load of roasted vegetables and gravy.

Chicken is fantastically versatile – whether it's the whole bird or specific bits of it. I love using thighs in particular: the cheeks of meat on the bone are so succulent and always retain their juiciness (even in slow-cooked one-pot dishes that have been on the stove for hours and hours by the time Gordon and I get to eat). On a practical level, too, thighs are the most economical cut to buy.

Although chicken in any form is one of my favourite speedy ingredients for weeknight meals, duck is a delicious alternative – and one that's no longer such a luxury now that it has become more readily available. Duck might be a tiny bit pricier than chicken, but it's just as easy to cook and is a tasty and impressive dish to serve to friends or family. I like to leave the skin on when cooking it because, although duck is a lean healthy option, the fat that is released during cooking keeps it beautifully moist. You can always remove the skin once it's cooked. I think the main ingredient of a dish should always be its focus and it doesn't need to be disguised with other flavours; it should just be simply prepared in order to bring out its delicious taste.

Gremolata chicken

Lemon chicken stew

Stuffed chicken breasts with
  mozzarella and basil

Coq au vin

Chinese duck stir-fry

Chicken and mushroom pie pots

Indian-style chicken kebabs

Roast chicken with chilli, garlic
  and lemon

Duck breasts with blackcurrant sauce

Gremolata chicken

This is unbelievably quick and simple but the results are delicious. I usually serve it with roasted new potatoes and lots more salad.

2 boneless, skinless chicken
   breasts
1 egg white
2 tbsp olive oil
2 handfuls of rocket leaves
1 lemon, cut into wedges,
   to serve
black pepper

FOR THE PASTE
leaves from 40g pack of fresh
   flat-leaf parsley
1 tbsp capers in vinegar,
   drained and rinsed
1 plump garlic clove, peeled
   and crushed
grated zest and juice of
   $1/2$ lemon
1 tbsp extra virgin olive oil

Serves: 2
Prep time: 15 minutes
Cooking time: 25 minutes
plus at least 20 minutes
marinating

1 Combine all the paste ingredients and season with pepper. I think the quickest way of doing this is to use a hand-held blender, but a knife and chopping board does just as well.

2 Score the top of the chicken breasts diagonally several times at about 2cm/$3/4$ inch intervals and 5mm/ $1/4$ inch deep. Brush with the egg white, then smear the paste into the chicken and push down into the scored slits to form a crust, pressing firmly to compact. Cover with cling film and place in the fridge for anything between 20 minutes and 2 hours.

3 When you are ready to cook the chicken, preheat the oven to 180°C/350°F/GM4, then heat the olive oil in a non-stick, ovenproof frying pan on a low-medium heat. Carefully place the chicken breasts, scored side down, in the shimmering oil and fry for 5 minutes. Turn the chicken over and cook for a further 5 minutes. Turn the chicken over again and cook in the oven for 10–15 minutes until cooked through.

4 Remove from the pan and cut the chicken into slices along the existing cuts. Arrange the chicken slices on the rocket and serve with the lemon wedges to squeeze over.

Lemon chicken stew

This is a very straightforward dish that takes only an hour or so to cook once you have chopped up all the vegetables. It's ideal for an informal, stress-free Saturday lunch with friends, served with plain brown rice and a crunchy salad. I have given ingredients for four people, but it's easy to make in bulk for a larger group.

3 tbsp olive oil
4 chicken drumsticks
4 chicken thighs
1 medium onion, peeled and diced
3 carrots, peeled and diced to same size as the onion
2 sticks of celery, diced to same size as the onion
2 garlic cloves, peeled and crushed
400g tin of chopped tomatoes
400ml/14fl oz chicken stock
1 red chilli, left whole
2 bay leaves
400g tin of cannellini beans, drained through a sieve and then rinsed
20g pack each of fresh flat-leaf parsley and coriander, leaves roughly chopped
zest and juice of 1 lemon
salt and black pepper

1 Warm the oil in a large enamel casserole dish with a tight-fitting lid on a medium heat and gently brown the chicken pieces on all sides, skin side first. When they are a rich golden colour, remove and put to one side.

2 Add the onion, carrots and celery and fry in the oil until just beginning to soften. Add the garlic and stir for a further minute, then return the chicken pieces to the casserole.

3 Pour in the tomatoes and stock and bring to the boil. Pop the whole chilli and bay leaves into the casserole and, using a spoon, push them under the surface of the liquid. Season with salt and pepper. Put on the lid, reduce the heat to low and simmer for 20 minutes. Stir in the cannellini beans, replace the lid and cook for a further 20 minutes.

4 When the cooking time is up, stir in the chopped parsley and coriander, the lemon zest and lemon juice. Serve immediately in warm flat bowls.

WHY NOT TRY...

With any leftovers, take the chicken off the bone and serve the stew with a baked potato.

Serves: 4
Prep time: 30 minutes
Cooking time: about 1 hour 10 minutes

Stuffed chicken breasts with mozzarella and basil

This is a very easy but impressive dish, simple, tasty and fresh. I love chicken Kiev but find this a little more exciting and slightly less potent.

1 tsp olive oil plus extra for greasing and drizzling
2 boneless, skinless chicken breasts
3 baby vine tomatoes
40g/1¹/₂oz mozzarella cheese
1 tsp chopped capers
sprig of fresh basil, torn
1 egg, beaten
75g/3oz dried breadcrumbs
salt and black pepper

Serves: 2
Prep time: 20 minutes
Cooking time: 20 minutes

1 Preheat the oven to 190°C/375°F/GM5. Lightly grease an oven tray.

2 Slit the chicken breasts open horizontally to make a pocket, being careful not to cut all the way through.

3 Place the tomatoes, mozzarella, capers and basil in a bowl, drizzle over the oil and add a grinding of black pepper and salt to taste.

4 Fill each chicken breast with the mixture, close the pocket and secure with a cocktail stick.

5 Pour the beaten egg into a large flattish bowl ready to dip the breasts into. Tip the breadcrumbs onto a large plate or tray. Coat the chicken breasts with the beaten egg, then turn them in the breadcrumbs, ensuring all sides are evenly coated (see Why Not Try...). Drizzle a little oil over both sides of the stuffed breasts.

6 Place the chicken breasts on the oven tray and bake in the oven for about 20 minutes, turning over halfway through cooking, until golden brown. Ensure the chicken is cooked through. Remove the cocktail sticks and serve.

WHY NOT TRY...

This is a great dish to make in advance and leave in the fridge for a few hours once you have coated the chicken. The breadcrumbs tend to stick better if they are refrigerated at this stage.

Serve with a rocket salad simply dressed with balsamic vinaigrette for a delicious main course.

I've always liked eating outdoors, whether in the garden at home or out on a picnic, as there's something really casual and laid back about this kind of food. So if the weather's dry and not too cold, we'll take our food outside. The children love having picnics – even if it's just in the garden – and they're much more relaxed, too, so it's a good time to introduce them to new foods that they might not otherwise eat. I find children are more adventurous if they are eating with their fingers, and it's a great excuse to ditch the cutlery.

I have to confess that I'm not a great fan of barbecues, though, because in my experience the food always seems to end up overcooked or burnt. There's a definite knack to barbecuing, and it's all to do with getting the heat at the right temperature, so I tend to leave it to the experts (like my South African brother-in-law, Jonty). What I mean by eating outdoors is having simple meat, chicken, or fish dishes with salads, or cold food that can be served without having to keep going in and out of the kitchen.

Chilled gazpacho soups, salads, quiches and pâtés can all be prepared ahead and served Mediterranean-style alongside platters of sliced meats, grilled vegetables, cheeses and fresh bread. It's a brilliant, informal kind of lunch that can be slapped on a board and left on the table for friends or family to help themselves. This is what lazy, hazy summer days are all about – the kids running around in the sunshine while we sit back and watch, casually picking at the food in front of us with no need to rush.

Coq au vin

Maybe there is a reason why a recipe becomes a cliché – it's so delicious that it's cooked far too often. For me, the combination of bacon, chicken, mushrooms and baby onions, slowly cooked in red wine, will always be a winner. That's why I think recipes like this need to be dusted off and handed on to the next generation. This is how I've always made it.

1 medium chicken, weighing about 1.4kg/3lb, jointed into 6 pieces, then breasts cut in half (or 2 breasts, cut in half widthways, plus 2 thighs and 2 drumsticks)

25g/1oz butter

1 tbsp olive oil

300g/11oz shallots, peeled (see Why Not Try...)

150g/5oz rashers of unsmoked streaky bacon, cut into small slices

1 garlic clove, peeled and crushed

1 rounded tbsp plain flour

200ml/7fl oz red wine

300ml/10fl oz chicken stock (or 300ml/10fl oz water with a good-quality chicken stock cube)

250g/9oz button mushrooms, stalks trimmed

4 sprigs of thyme, tied together with kitchen string

salt and pepper

20g pack of fresh flat-leaf parsley, stalks removed and leaves roughly chopped, to serve

1 Start by marinating the chicken. I think the easiest way is to put the chicken joints, carrot, celery, bruised garlic clove and bay leaves into a large freezer bag. Pour over the wine. Squeeze out any excess air and fasten the bag as tightly as possible with a wire tie. Put the bag into a bowl large enough to accommodate it easily, to make sure none of the marinade leaks over your fridge. Place the bowl in the fridge overnight. Whenever you remember, turn the bag around in the bowl to make sure all the flavours mix together well.

2 When you are ready to start cooking, preheat the oven to 170°C/325°F/GM3.

3 Melt the butter and oil in a large cast-iron casserole dish with a tight-fitting lid on a medium heat on the hob. Add the shallots and bacon and fry until brown. Using a slotted spoon, remove the shallots and bacon and put to one side.

4 Carefully remove the chicken from the bag of marinade. Discard the bruised garlic clove but reserve the rest of the marinade. Dry the chicken with absorbent kitchen paper. Carefully place the chicken pieces, skin-side down, in the hot fat in the casserole and fry until browned all over, turning as necessary. Depending on the size of your pan, you may have to do this in batches. When the chicken is evenly browned, return all the pieces to the casserole, add the bacon and shallots and stir in the crushed garlic.

FOR THE MARINADE

2 carrots, peeled and halved
  lengthways
1 stick of celery, halved
1 garlic clove, peeled and
  bruised
2 bay leaves
300ml/10fl oz red wine

Serves: 4
Prep time: 40 minutes plus
marinating overnight
Cooking time: about 1¹/₄ hours

WHY NOT TRY...

**The easiest way to peel
shallots is to pour boiling
water over them, leave for
1 minute, then drain and peel.**

**Defy tradition and leave in
the carrot and celery pieces.
Though soft, they taste
delicious.**

5 Reduce the heat, then sprinkle the flour over the
chicken, bacon and shallots and stir into the fat. Fry
for a minute or so, then add the wine, chicken stock
and the wine from the marinade. Stir well. Add the
carrot and celery pieces from the marinade bag and
push under the liquid. Stir in the mushrooms and
add the thyme. Lightly season with salt and pepper.

6 Bring to the boil, put on the lid and transfer to the
oven for 50 minutes, removing after 25 minutes to
baste the chicken with the gravy.

7 When the cooking time is complete, remove the
thyme, bay leaves, celery and carrot pieces and discard.
Skim off any fat from the surface of the dish and check
the seasoning. Serve on warm plates, sprinkled with
parsley.

Chinese duck stir-fry

This is a simple, quick supper – you can put lots more into this dish, such as mushrooms or baby corn, but I have kept this really easy. The nice part is that you can empty out the bottom of your vegetable and salad drawer of odds and ends when you do a stir-fry, which is really handy, and all you need to buy is a lovely duck or chicken breast.

1 whole duck breast
1 tbsp runny honey
200g/7oz egg noodles
1 tbsp sesame oil
1 tbsp olive oil
1 red chilli, deseeded and
    finely chopped
1 garlic clove, peeled and
    finely chopped
3cm/1¼ inch piece of fresh
    root ginger, peeled and cut
    into thin strips
1 handful of baby carrots
1 handful of sugar snap peas
1 red pepper, deseeded and
    cut into long strips
5 spring onions, cut into
    long strips
2 tbsp mirin
2 tbsp dark soy sauce
1 small handful of fresh
    coriander leaves, plus the
    stalks, finely chopped
salt and black pepper

Serves: 2 generously
Prep time: 20 minutes
Cooking time: about
30 minutes

1 Preheat the oven to 180°C/350°F/GM4.

2 Season the duck with salt and pepper. Score the skin of the duck breast and place it, skin side down, in a cold ovenproof frying pan. Set this on a medium heat and gently fry without moving the breast around until the skin has browned. Turn the breast over and drizzle the honey over the skin, gently rubbing the honey into the slits with the back of a teaspoon. When the underside has browned, place in the oven for 5–8 minutes, depending on the thickness of the duck breast. Remove and leave to rest for 5 minutes, then cut into thin slices.

3 Cook the noodles as instructed on the packet and leave to drain. Toss with 1 teaspoon of the sesame oil to prevent them sticking.

4 Heat the olive oil and remaining sesame oil in a wok or large frying pan. Add the chilli, garlic and ginger and stir-fry for 1 minute over a medium-high heat. Add the carrots and sugar snap peas, red pepper and spring onions and stir-fry for 3–4 minutes, until beginning to soften. Pour over half the mirin and soy sauce and stir-fry for 2–3 minutes longer.

5 Add the noodles and coriander stalks to the vegetables, plus the remaining mirin and soy sauce, and toss together so that the mirin and soy sauce coats everything.

6 Spoon into warm bowls, fan the duck pieces over the top and sprinkle with the coriander leaves.

Chicken and mushroom pie pots

I really like making individual pies and the kids love having their own – let's face it, you don't get someone stealing all your favourite filling bits! Try making them in large ramekins for children with smaller appetites. If you prefer, you can, of course, just make one big pie.

4 boneless, skinless chicken breasts, sliced into 1cm/ ¹/₂ inch wide strips
3 tbsp olive oil
2 red onions, peeled and finely sliced
2 garlic cloves, peeled and finely chopped
12 button mushrooms, sliced
2 tsp fresh tarragon leaves
50ml/2fl oz white wine
200ml/7fl oz fresh chicken stock
142ml carton of double cream
2 tbsp chopped fresh flat-leaf parsley
375g pack of ready-rolled puff pastry
1 egg, lightly beaten
salt and black pepper

Serves: 4
Prep time: 50 minutes
Cooking time: about 50 minutes

1 Preheat the oven to 180°C/350°F/GM4.

2 Season the chicken with salt and pepper. Heat 2 tablespoons of the oil in a large frying pan and brown the chicken pieces on all sides. Take out and put to one side.

3 Add the remaining oil to the pan, then add the onions and garlic and cook until softened. Add the mushrooms and tarragon and cook until the mushrooms are tender and lightly coloured. Pour in the wine and simmer until almost evaporated, then add the stock and simmer until reduced by half.

4 Add the cream and simmer for a couple of minutes, until the sauce is slightly thickened, then add the parsley and season with salt and pepper. Leave to cool. *con't.*

WHY NOT TRY...

You can make the filling in advance and leave in the pie dishes in the fridge. You will need to cook the pies for slightly longer to make sure the filling is thoroughly heated through, and you may need to cover the tops with foil to prevent them getting too brown.

Serve with a large side dish of steamed broccoli and delicious new potatoes.

5 Stir the chicken into the thickened sauce. Divide the mixture between four ovenproof bowls, each about 300ml/10fl oz capacity; the mixture should reach about 1cm/$\frac{1}{2}$ inch from the top (see Why Not Try...).

6 Divide the sheet of pastry into four and cut a strip from each piece about 1cm/$\frac{1}{2}$ inch wide. Brush the rim of each pie dish with the beaten egg, then gently press the pastry strips around each rim. Next, take the pastry squares and lay them over the top of the pie, trimming off any excess pastry. Using your thumb and forefinger, pinch around the rim of each pie at 2cm/$\frac{3}{4}$ inch intervals to seal. Make a small hole in the centre of each one.

7 Lightly brush the tops with beaten egg and add a light sprinkling of salt. If you are feeling artistic, use the pastry trimmings to decorate the tops with cut-out pastry shapes and stick them on with beaten egg.

8 Place the pies onto an oven tray and bake in the oven for 25–30 minutes until piping hot in the centre and golden brown on the top.

Indian-style chicken kebabs

This recipe is a wonderful summer barbeque dish, but can equally be made for a quick and simple evening supper, served with rice and salad. The longer the chicken marinates the better, so ideally it would sit in the marinade in the fridge for a day or overnight, but I have also made the whole dish from scratch in an evening and it tasted delicious. The results are definitely best and easiest to achieve if you use a microplane grater.

2 large boneless, skinless chicken
   breasts, cut into 2cm/^{3}/$_4$ inch cubes
1 lemon, cut into wedges to serve

FOR THE MARINADE
1 tsp coriander seeds, crushed
5cm/2 inch piece of fresh root ginger,
   peeled and grated
3 plump garlic cloves, peeled and
   grated
1 red chilli, deseeded and finely sliced
2 tsp garam masala
2 tbsp Greek yoghurt
zest and juice of 1 lemon

FOR THE YOGHURT DRESSING
1 small onion, peeled and grated
   to produce about 1 dspn of onion
   gloop
2 heaped tbsp Greek yoghurt
2 tbsp chopped fresh coriander
1 tbsp chopped fresh mint
squeeze of lemon juice
salt and pepper

Serves: 2
Prep time: 30 minutes plus marinating
Cooking time: 15-20 minutes

1 Start by making the marinade. Combine all the marinade ingredients in a bowl and add the chopped chicken. Stir well, making sure the chicken is well coated. Cover and leave in the fridge for as long as possible, ideally overnight.

2 When ready to cook, preheat the oven to 200°C/400°F/GM6. Soak 4 × 30.5cm/12 inch wooden skewers in cold water for 30 minutes.

3 Remove the chicken pieces from the marinade and divide evenly between the skewers. Cook in the oven for 15-20 minutes or, if you prefer, barbeque for about 15 minutes (making sure they are cooked through). Halfway through the cooking, turn the kebabs and baste them with the remaining marinade.

4 The yoghurt dressing can be made a little in advance, but is easy enough to prepare while the chicken is cooking. Mix the grated onion with the yoghurt and chopped herbs and season with a squeeze of lemon juice and salt and pepper.

5 Check the chicken is thoroughly cooked by slicing into the thickest chunk of chicken. If there is no pinkness to the meat and it is piping hot, the chicken is ready.

6 Arrange the kebabs on two serving plates and serve with lemon wedges and the sauce on the side.

The busiest time of my day is usually between 4.00pm and 8.30pm. There is dinner and homework, baths and reading to get through before I can even think of sitting down without having any demands being made on me.

The time when the children are in bed marks the end of one part of the day and the start of another – usually one when I can get on with all the other stuff I haven't managed to do while they've been around. If I haven't eaten with the children, I'll have my dinner to cook and this will always be quick and simple so that I can get on with reading and replying to emails, returning phone calls, or simply curling up in front of the television to catch up on programmes I've missed.

If Gordon's home the pattern of the evening is much the same, but instead of working we'll spend time together. Evenings are precious for everyone, but I find that's particularly so when you're a parent. I think it's really important for parents to have time to themselves and with other adults without the children. Whether it's your partner, your friends, or your family, every relationship needs working at, not just those with your kids. Parenting is a full-time job, but we all deserve a little time off every now and again to be ourselves.

Roast chicken with chilli, garlic and lemon

Roast chicken is one of our favourite meals at home, I tend to cook it at least twice a week, even if it is just to have in the fridge as a standby for a quick lunch or sandwich filling. There are so many different herbs and spices that you can match with it when roasting but this is a favourite.

1 large chicken
olive oil
2 red chillies, deseeded and
  finely chopped
2 cloves of garlic, finely chopped
1 lemon, $1/2$ to squeeze and
  $1/2$ thinly sliced
balsamic vinegar
4 knobs of butter
sea salt

Serves: 6
Prep and cooking times:
about $1^1/2$ hours depending on
the size of your chicken

1 Preheat the oven to 200°C/400°F/GM6.

2 Place the chicken in a roasting dish, drizzle oil over the top and sprinkle with the chillies and garlic. Squeeze lemon juice over the chicken and place the lemon slices around the leg and cavity area. Place the squeezed lemon half in the cavity. Season the chicken with salt, drizzle some balsamic vinegar over and cover with foil.

3 Place in the oven for 20 minutes per 500g/1lb 2oz plus 25 minutes. I always remove the foil for the last 25 minutes and dot the knobs of butter onto the top for extra flavour and to really crisp up the skin. You can also drizzle with extra oil if you like.

4 When you take the chicken from the oven, test with a skewer to check the juices are running clear and then let it stand for about 15 minutes before serving. Discard any bits of chilli that have overbrowned.

Duck breasts with blackcurrant sauce

This is an unbelievably quick after-work supper that can be ready from scratch within 30 minutes of walking through the front door. If you're really hungry, serve with a watercress salad and smooth and creamy garlicky mash.

2 duck breasts, skin on
150ml/5fl oz red wine
150g/5oz good-quality
    blackcurrant jam
1 tbsp crème de Cassis
    (optional)
salt and black pepper

Serves: 2
Prep time: 5 minutes
Cooking time: 15–20 minutes

1 Preheat the oven to 220°C/425°F/GM7.

2 Score the skin of each duck breast several times, then place on a non-stick baking tray and season with salt and pepper. Cook in the oven for 15–20 minutes.

3 While the duck is cooking, put the wine, blackcurrant jam and crème de Cassis, if using, in a saucepan and bring to the boil. Reduce the heat and simmer for 10–15 minutes. The sauce should be reduced and syrupy. Season to taste. Remove from the heat and put to one side until the duck is ready.

4 Remove the duck from the oven. For a healthier option, as soon as it is cool enough to handle, peel off the skin and discard. Cut each breast diagonally into slices about 1cm/^{1}/$_2$ inch thick.

5 Arrange the duck on warm plates and drizzle over plenty of the sauce.

Simply
BEEF

I have to confess that we are real meat-eaters in our house, particularly Gordon, and beef is one ingredient that makes a frequent appearance on our plates.

We're both great believers in knowing where our food has come from, and we feel that the children should know this, too. Growing up on a farm meant that every day I had to come in through the back door past a load of rabbits hanging up from a shoot. But this didn't put me off eating meat, and it doesn't bother our children either. In fact, while Gordon was filming 'The F Word' recently, Jack, our son, went along to catch rabbits and he happily helped his dad to skin and eat one.

Veal has, unfortunately, become unpopular because of a lot of bad press about the inhumane way that calves are treated abroad, which is a shame because veal is absolutely delicious. If your reason for not eating veal is because you are concerned for the welfare of the animals, go to your butcher or supermarket counter and ask about its traceability. The recipe for stuffed veal wraps in this chapter is simple and tastes fantastic. As with the Thai beef green curry, and many other recipes in this book, it was inspired by a dish we'd eaten while on a family holiday. Our eight-year-old daughter, Holly, picked this out when we stopped for lunch in a fantastic deli in the States.

Sesame beef salad

Carpaccio of beef with Parmesan
  and rocket

Stuffed veal wraps

Perfect telly-supper steak sandwich

Fillet steak gratin

Thai beef green curry

Old-fashioned, amazingly delicious lasagne

Beef Rendang

Cinnamon beef stew

Beef stir-fry with noodles

Sesame beef salad

This is very straightforward. The colours look wonderful, and the taste is fresh and crunchy. This really does taste better the longer you are able to marinate the beef. A couple of hours at room temperature would be fine, but up to 24 hours in the fridge would be wonderful. Serve with fresh bread.

1 × 600g/1lb 5oz rump steak

3 tbsp sesame seeds

1 orange and 1 red pepper, quartered, deseeded and finely sliced lengthways

1 fennel bulb, trimmed, quartered and finely sliced lengthways

1 small red onion, peeled and finely sliced

1 Romaine lettuce

1 bunch of watercress

20g pack of fresh coriander

6 spring onions, green parts discarded, white parts finely sliced lengthways

1 tbsp sesame oil

1 Begin by mixing together all the marinade ingredients. Place the steak in a medium freezer bag and pour in the marinade. Make sure all sides of the beef are coated in the marinade, then squeeze out any air from the bag. Tie the bag tightly and leave to marinate for as long as possible. Every so often, turn the bag over so that all the beef has a turn at soaking thoroughly.

2 Warm a non-stick frying pan on a medium heat. Add the sesame seeds and toast until they are medium brown. They will burn very easily, so don't take your eyes off them while they are cooking. As soon as they are the right colour, pour onto a plate and put to one side for later.

3 In a large mixing bowl, combine the sliced peppers, fennel and red onion. If you are making this slightly in advance, cover with cold water to keep them fresh and crisp. *cont.*

FOR THE MARINADE

2.5cm/1 inch piece of fresh
    root ginger, peeled and
    thinly sliced
3 garlic cloves, peeled and
    thinly sliced
juice of 3 limes
4 tbsp soy sauce
3 tbsp olive oil
1 tbsp sesame oil

Serves 6 as first course,
4 as main course
Prep time: 30 minutes plus
at least 2 hours marinating
Cooking time: 6 minutes

4 Wash the lettuce, watercress and coriander leaves and dry well. Tear the lettuce leaves roughly.

5 About 20 minutes before you are ready to eat, heat the frying pan until it is very hot. Remove the steak from the marinade, picking off any bits clinging to it and reserving the marinade. Carefully add the steak to the pan and cook for 3 minutes, then turn it over and cook for a further 3 minutes. Transfer to a plate and put to one side for 10 minutes to rest.

6 Reduce the heat to low and carefully pour the reserved marinade through a sieve into the pan. Bring to the boil, stirring, and simmer for 1 minute.

7 When the steak has rested, cut off any fat and thinly slice the meat. Add any juices from the beef to the cooked marinade. Put the sliced beef into a mixing bowl and pour over the cooked marinade and toasted sesame seeds. Stir well.

8 Take a large, fairly flat serving dish and put about one-third of the lettuce, coriander and watercress onto it. Now add a third of the pepper mixture and, finally, sprinkle with a third of the beef. Repeat this process until everything is on the serving plate. Garnish with the spring onions, pour over any remaining marinade and drizzle with the sesame oil. Serve immediately with fresh, crusty bread to mop up the juices.

Carpaccio of beef with Parmesan and rocket

This is a very expensive dish and one that I really love as a treat. It is very impressive to look at and surprisingly easy to do. Not for the usual family meal, but when you really want to push the boat out why not try it?

olive oil for brushing
2 tbsp black peppercorns, crushed
1 × 500g/1lb 2oz fillet of beef, well trimmed
2 tbsp chopped fresh flat-leaf parsley
50g/2oz rocket leaves
freshly shaved Parmesan cheese

FOR THE DRESSING
$^1/_2$ tsp runny honey, warmed
1 tbsp lemon juice
$1^1/_2$ tsp white wine vinegar
$^1/_2$ tsp wholegrain mustard
5 tbsp olive oil
salt

1 Brush a large piece of foil with a little oil and scatter the crushed peppercorns into the centre.

2 Roll the beef in the peppercorns until evenly coated. Wrap the fillet in foil and secure the ends tightly. Let this rest in the fridge for at least 30 minutes.

3 Heat a frying pan over a very high heat and sear the foil packet for 20–30 seconds on each side. Leave this to cool, then put into the freezer for at least 1 hour. This will make it easier to slice.

4 Meanwhile, make the dressing. Put the honey into a bowl and whisk in the lemon juice, vinegar and mustard, then whisk in the oil. Season to taste with salt.

5 Unwrap the beef and roll it in the chopped parsley, then cut into incredibly thin slices – you need an extremely sharp knife.

6 Toss the rocket in enough dressing to coat it lightly. Arrange the beef on individual plates in overlapping slices. Pile the rocket in the centre, drizzle the remaining dressing over the beef and scatter the Parmesan shavings over. Serve.

Serves: 6 as a starter
Prep time: 20 minutes plus $1^1/_2$ hours chilling
Cooking time: 5 minutes

Friday nights are lovely, happy evenings in our house; they mark the end of a long week and the start of a lazy weekend. We all have such busy weekday schedules that we like to do as little as possible on Saturday and Sunday.

The house rule is that homework has to be cleared out of the way on Friday night, so it's not hanging over everyone for the rest of the weekend. Once the work's out of the way the television will often go on and we can all start to wind down together. The children are allowed to stay up later than usual.

As I like to make Friday a sort of night off for me, too, dinner will always be something simple and speedy that can be put together with the minimum of effort. Occasionally we'll treat ourselves to a take-away, but more often I'll cook the family's favourite comfort food – some form of beef. We love supper in front of the telly with a steak sandwich each or beef steaks with home-made chunky chips and a fresh green salad. Both these dishes make a quick, easy supper that requires no effort to throw together, clear up after, or eat – especially with the children mucking in, peeling potatoes and stacking the dishwasher. There's no better way to start the weekend.

Stuffed veal wraps

This is a really interesting meal – I had it on a trip to the States. We went into a deli for lunch and Holly spotted this at the deli counter and decided to choose it for her lunch – we all ended up wishing we had done the same, it is delicious! I think I have got it right, but could only get the recipe by dissecting her lunch, which as you can imagine does not go down well with a hungry eight year old!

4 × 140g/4^{1}/$_{2}$oz veal escalopes
4 tbsp finely chopped fresh flat-leaf parsley
2 balls of mozzarella, sliced
1 garlic clove, peeled and finely chopped
200g/7oz marinated red and yellow peppers, sliced into thin strips
12 slices of thinly sliced pancetta
3 tbsp olive oil
salt and black pepper
rocket leaves to serve

FOR THE DRESSING
1 tbsp balsamic vinegar
4 tbsp olive oil
1 tsp grain mustard
salt and black pepper to taste

Serves: 4
Prep time: 20 minutes
Cooking time: 15 minutes

1 Preheat the oven to 180°C/350°F/GM4.

2 Lay out the veal escalopes on a board. Start by sprinkling over the parsley, then salt and a grinding of black pepper to taste. Add a layer of mozzarella, then the garlic and peppers. Roll up each escalope and wrap the pancetta around, then secure them in a roll with a couple of cocktail sticks.

3 Heat the oil in an ovenproof frying pan and get to a shimmering heat. Add the wraps to the pan and fry until they are nice and golden and the pancetta is crispy. The mozzarella should be melting inside as well. Pop the pan in the oven and cook for a further 10 minutes.

4 Meanwhile, mix the dressing ingredients and toss the rocket leaves with the dressing in a large bowl. Arrange on a serving plate and serve immediately with a piping hot veal wrap on top.

Perfect telly-supper steak sandwich

There are many versions of the steak sandwich and, no doubt, everyone has their own views. But, for me, this is the very best way of preparing steak to be eaten in front of the telly without need of knives or forks. Perhaps a napkin would be a good idea, though!

1 × 400g/14oz sirloin steak
2 tbsp olive oil
1 oven-ready loaf of ciabatta
    bread
juice of $^{1}/_{2}$ lemon
1 tsp balsamic vinegar
2 tsp Dijon mustard
1 generous handful of rocket
    leaves
salt and black pepper
tomato ketchup to serve
    (optional)

Serves: 2
Prep time: 15 minutes, plus
at least 30 minutes marinating
Cooking time: 10 minutes
plus resting

1 It is very important that the steak is at room temperature before you start to cook it. So, begin by removing the meat from the fridge and put it in a shallow dish. Coat the steak on all sides with the oil and a good grinding of pepper. Leave for at least 30 minutes. Meanwhile, heat the oven as instructed on the ciabatta packet.

2 When the meat is ready and you are ready to eat, put the ciabatta in the oven and cook as instructed on the packet – usually about 10 minutes. Heat a non-stick frying pan on a medium to hot heat and wait for it to be really hot. Season the steak with salt, then carefully put it in the pan and cook for 3 minutes. Turn it over and cook for a further 3 minutes, then remove from the pan and place on a flat dish. Leave for 10 minutes to rest.

3 When the steak has rested, transfer to a chopping board, making sure to save all the meat juices. Using a very sharp knife, cut away all the fat from the steak to leave you with a perfect piece of lean, rare meat. Cut the steak diagonally into very fine ribbons and put in a medium-sized mixing bowl. Pour over all the cooking juices and the lemon juice and balsamic vinegar.

4 Cut the ciabatta loaf into two pieces and slice in half horizontally. Spread the bottom half of the warm bread with the mustard. Add the rocket leaves to the sliced steak and toss well, using all the lemony steak juices as a dressing. Pile the steak and rocket into the bread and eat immediately with a dollop of ketchup if required.

Fillet steak gratin

A perfect supper for two, when the kids are in bed.

2 × 300g/11oz fillet steaks
4 tbsp olive oil
2 knobs of butter
2 large handfuls of field
   mushrooms, quartered
2 tbsp crème fraîche
2 egg yolks
2 tbsp chopped fresh chives
2 tsp wholegrain mustard
2 handfuls of grated
   Parmesan cheese
salt and black pepper
rocket salad to serve

Serves: 2
Prep time: 10 minutes
Cooking time: 5 minutes

1 Preheat the grill to high.

2 Season the fillet steaks with salt and pepper. Heat an ovenproof frying pan with 2 tablespoons of the oil until smoking, then sear the steaks on all sides. Fry for 2 minutes on each side (for medium rare), or until cooked to your liking. Finish with a knob of butter and remove the pan from the heat.

3 Heat the remaining oil in a separate pan. Add the mushrooms and fry over a medium to high heat until cooked through. Season to taste, then spoon the mushrooms into a small bowl and put to one side.

4 In a bowl, mix the crème fraîche with the egg yolk, chives, mustard and Parmesan until well combined. Fold in the mushrooms, then spoon the mixture on top of the fillet steaks and cook under the grill for 5 minutes, or until the topping is golden and bubbling.

5 Serve with rocket salad on the side.

WHY NOT TRY...

Perfect served with warm crusty bread.

Thai beef green curry

This is a version of a delicious curry we had recently in Thailand. I had the skeleton recipe and it took a couple of tries before I got it right, but a good friend of mine, Karen, finally came up trumps and we got this amazingly quick and easy version!

1 tbsp sunflower oil

2.5cm/1 inch piece of fresh
  root ginger, peeled and
  finely chopped

2 sticks of lemon grass, outer
  layers discarded and
  finely sliced

2 tbsp Thai green curry paste

600g/1lb 5oz sirloin steak, fat
  removed and steak thinly
  sliced and cut into strips

400ml tin of coconut milk

150g/5oz picked pea
  aubergines

6 fresh lime leaves

1 tbsp Thai fish sauce

1 tbsp caster sugar

100g/3^1/$_2$oz fine green beans,
  blanched

squeeze of lime juice

ripped small handful of Thai
  basil, to garnish

steamed Thai fragrant rice
  to serve

Serves: 3–4
Prep time: 10 minutes
Cooking time: about
20 minutes

1 Heat the oil in a large frying pan or wok. Sauté the ginger and lemon grass for 2 minutes, taking care not to colour. Stir in the curry paste and cook for a couple of minutes until the oil begins to run.

2 Add the steak strips and sauté for 2–3 minutes until sealed. Add the coconut milk, pea aubergines, lime leaves, fish sauce and sugar. Give it a good stir and simmer for 10–15 minutes, stirring occasionally and taking care not to let it catch on the bottom of the pan.

3 Just before serving, stir in the green beans to heat through, along with a squeeze of lime juice. Serve with steaming hot Thai fragrant rice and the Thai basil sprinkled on the top.

WHY NOT TRY...

If you can't get hold of pea aubergines, use diced courgettes, sweet potatoes or butternut squash instead.

You can use dried lime leaves if you can't get hold of them fresh, but they aren't quite as flavoursome.

Thai supermarkets always stock pea aubergines and frozen fresh lime leaves.

Old-fashioned, amazingly delicious lasagne

This may take ages to make but it is so worth it – not the healthiest, but we all deserve a good old indulgent treat!

140g/4$^{1}/_{2}$oz chopped pancetta
2 onions, peeled and chopped
1 garlic clove, peeled and
　chopped
1 carrot, peeled and chopped
2 sticks of celery, finely chopped
1.5kg/3lb 5oz beef mince
1 tbsp soy sauce
2 tbsp Worcester sauce
black pepper
375ml/13fl oz full-fat milk
40g/1$^{1}/_{2}$oz butter
400ml/14fl oz beef stock
225ml/8fl oz dry red wine
400g/14oz tomato purée
1 handful of fresh basil
8 fresh lasagne sheets
160g/5$^{1}/_{2}$oz Parmesan
　cheese, grated

FOR THE WHITE SAUCE
125g/4oz butter
100g/3$^{1}/_{2}$oz plain flour
1.3 litres/2$^{1}/_{4}$ pints hot milk
salt and black pepper

Serves: 8–10
Prep time: 1 hour
Cooking time: 2$^{1}/_{2}$ hours

1　Fry the pancetta in a large pan. Add the onions and garlic and fry until softened but not coloured. Add the carrot and celery and sweat for 10–15 minutes. Add the beef, soy sauce, Worcester sauce and a good grinding of black pepper and break it up, then fry on a medium heat until browned. Add the milk and butter and cook to reduce by half. Stir in the stock, wine and tomato purée. Simmer, uncovered, for at least 1 hour, then finely chop the basil, add to the pan and cook for a further 30 minutes.

2　To make the white sauce, melt the butter in a pan. Add the flour and stir to a paste, then leave to bubble for a minute or two until really dry. Gradually stir in the hot milk, allow it to come to the boil and stir until the sauce thickens. Check the seasoning and take off the heat.

3　Preheat the oven to 200°C/400°F/GM6.

4　Lightly grease a deep 25.5 × 35.5cm/10 × 14 inch ovenproof dish, then spread a layer of the meat sauce over the base, about 1cm/$^{1}/_{2}$ inch deep. Lay pasta sheets on top, then spoon on the white sauce to a depth of 1cm/$^{1}/_{2}$ inch, followed by a sprinkling of Parmesan. Repeat the layering until you have used up all your ingredients, finishing with white sauce on the top and the last of the Parmesan.

5　Bake in the oven for 40–45 minutes until the top is bubbling and golden brown – don't worry about it bubbling over the sides, this is the look of an authentic lasagne! Delicious served with a crunchy green salad and garlic bread.

Beef Rendang

Beef Rendang certainly won't win any beauty prizes, but it tastes amazing and is even better if made a day or two in advance. This recipe is based on an Indonesian classic where the beef is slowly simmered in coconut milk until the sauce has virtually disappeared. To make it look a little prettier, garnish with fresh coriander leaves and some thinly sliced red chilli and serve with lots of quartered limes to squeeze over and rice or noodles, depending on how you feel.

2 tbsp sunflower oil
1kg/2¼lb stewing steak
3 × 400ml tins of coconut milk
2 sticks of lemon grass, bruised
1 tbsp fish sauce

FOR THE PASTE
1 red onion
5cm/2 inch fresh root ginger
6 garlic cloves
1 red pepper
4 dried red chillies
2 tsp ground coriander
2 tsp ground cinnamon
1 tsp ground cloves
1 tsp ground turmeric
50ml/2fl oz water

TO GARNISH AND SERVE
coriander leaves
1 mild red chilli, finely sliced
4 limes, quartered, to serve

Serves: 4
Prep time: 25 minutes
Cooking time: 2–2½ hours

1 First make the paste. Peel and chop the onion, ginger and garlic. Deseed and chop the red pepper and place in a food processor with all the remaining paste ingredients and blitz until completely smooth.

2 Cut the steak into 5cm/2 inch chunks

3 Heat the oil in a large wide casserole or saucepan and when it is hot, add the paste and stir for about 3 minutes until the smell of the spices fills the kitchen.

4 Add the steak and stir well, making sure that all the meat is coated with the paste. Pour in the coconut milk and stir well. Bring to the boil, then reduce the heat until the pot is simmering gently. Discard the outer layers of the lemon grass and bruise and add.

5 To begin with, this will need very little attention. However, after 1½–2 hours, as the sauce starts to thicken, it will be necessary to stir fairly regularly to make sure the sauce is not catching the bottom of the pan and burning. When the sauce is very thick and coats the meat, add the fish sauce. It may need a little more, depending upon your taste.

6 Remove from the heat and, if reheating at a later time, allow to cool completely before placing in the fridge until needed.

7 Serve garnished with plenty of coriander, sliced chilli (deseeded) and lime quarters.

Cinnamon beef stew

This is a real winter dish. The smell of the cinnamon fills the house and gets everyone excited about the meal to come. If you can get hold of baby carrots, that would be lovely, but it is not at all necessary for the flavour. Make a day in advance, if possible. Serve with mashed potato.

1kg/2¼lb braising steak, cut into 5cm/2 inch cubes
200ml/7fl oz marsala
2 medium onions, peeled and quartered
1 stick of celery, cut into chunks
2 garlic cloves, peeled
400g tin of chopped tomatoes
6 tbsp olive oil
300g/11oz shallots, peeled (see page 37)
350g/12oz baby carrots, scrubbed, topped and tailed, or large carrots, peeled and cut diagonally into 2.5cm/ 1 inch chunks
1 tbsp tomato purée
200ml/7fl oz water
2 bay leaves
2 large cinnamon sticks
250ml/9fl oz fresh beef stock
salt and black pepper

Serves: 4-6
Prep time: 40 minutes plus minimum 30 minutes marinating
Cooking time: 2½ hours

1 Put the beef into a mixing bowl and pour the marsala over it. Stir well to make sure the beef is separated and covered in wine. Cover and leave at room temperature for anything between 30 minutes and 2 hours.

2 Preheat the oven to 180°C/350°F/GM4.

3 Put the onions, celery and garlic into a food processor and blitz until completely smooth. (Or finely chop the vegetables by hand.) Add the tomatoes to the food processor and blitz again.

4 Remove the beef from the marsala marinade and dry on absorbent kitchen paper. Reserve the marinade for use later.

5 Heat half the oil on a high heat in a casserole with a tight-fitting lid until it shimmers. Add the beef in batches and brown on all sides. Transfer to a plate and put to one side. Add the remaining oil and cook the carrots and shallots until coloured at the edges. Return the beef to the casserole. Pour over the puréed vegetable and tomato mixture, then add the tomato purée, the reserved marinade and the water.

6 Bring to the boil, stirring all the time, then season with salt and pepper. Tuck the bay leaves and cinnamon sticks into the stew, making sure they are completely submerged in the liquid. Place in the oven and cook for 1 hour, then add the beef stock, season with salt and pepper and stir. Return to the oven and cook for a further 1½ hours or until the beef is tender. Check the seasoning before serving.

Beef stir-fry with noodles

This is very quick and easy, but tastes wonderful. The only preparation required is vegetable chopping, which is hardly difficult and the cooking takes minutes.

3 tbsp grapeseed oil
125g/4oz wok-ready noodles
1 red pepper, quartered,
    deseeded and thinly sliced
100g/3^1/$_2$oz green beans
1 bunch of spring onions,
    green parts removed and
    white parts finely sliced
    lengthways
2 garlic cloves, peeled and
    thinly sliced
2.5cm/1 inch piece of fresh
    root ginger, cut into the
    finest matchstick pieces
    possible
400g/14oz rump steak, fat
    removed and cut into
    3mm/^{1}/$_8$ inch slices
salt
1 lime, quartered, to serve

FOR THE SAUCE
50ml/2fl oz boiling water
^{1}/$_2$ beef stock cube
2 tbsp hoisin sauce
2 tbsp dry sherry
1 tsp soft dark brown sugar

1 Combine all the sauce ingredients in a cup. Stir well to make sure the stock cube and sugar have dissolved, then put to one side.

2 Heat a wok or large deep frying pan over a very high flame and add 1 tablespoon of the oil. When it starts to smoke, add the noodles and cook, stirring, for 1–2 minutes, until they have broken up. Transfer to a plate and put to one side.

3 Replace the pan on the heat and add another tablespoon of oil. Add the red pepper, beans and spring onions and stir-fry for about 2 minutes until they are hot and just starting to cook. Transfer to a plate and put to one side.

4 Put the pan back on the heat and add another tablespoon of oil. When the oil is smoking, add the garlic and ginger and toss in the oil for a few seconds, then add the steak. Stir round the pan for about 2 minutes until the meat is just sealed, but no more. Return the partially cooked vegetables to the pan and stir well. Throw in the cup of sauce ingredients and stir again.

5 Finally, return the noodles to the pan and stir well to make sure everything is evenly mixed together. Check the seasoning and, if necessary, add a little salt.

6 Serve in deep warm bowls with the lime wedges on the side.

Serves: 2
Prep time: 10 minutes
Cooking time: 8 minutes

While it is great to have activities and plans, it's also good to let children unwind and play among themselves. My children are really busy during term time and, as they get older and schoolwork becomes more demanding, I think it is even more important for them to be able to relax and let go of the pressure of school when they get home.

My Montessori training involved putting a lot of emphasis on allowing children to take the initiative during play; this teaches them to follow their natural curiosity and be active rather than passive learners. Letting children play by themselves teaches them independence and encourages them to use their imaginations; if you overfill their lives they may later find it difficult to motivate and amuse themselves. The classic phrases 'I'm bored' or 'I can't find anything to do' can drive you crazy when you know they have countless toys waiting to be played with.

So I make a point of building down-time into our lives by keeping weekends free and holidays as relaxed as possible. Having this 'home' time allows the children to have the freedom to play in their bedrooms, to play together, to use their own initiatives and amuse themselves. By letting them do this I find that they come up with much more imaginative games than I could ever suggest – usually involving simple things like a blanket, a box and a torch!

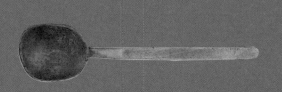

Simply
FISH & SEAFOOD

Our children are always in and out of the house – at school, playing sport, or whatever – so some days they are home late and end up eating dinner really close to their bedtime. On nights like that, I find giving them fish is ideal. It's quick and easy to prepare and light enough not to make them feel uncomfortable when they go to bed. And the kids love it. As they've got older, their tastes have changed and they will now happily eat more grown-up versions of fish dishes, rather than just fish pie and goujons (although both these still have their place as deliciously comforting foods).

Fish is such a healthy ingredient – it's low in fat and the oily varieties are packed with omega 3 – that I see it as a crucial part of the children's diet, so we will eat it once or twice a week. Salmon is a really good option because it can be roasted, poached, or pan-fried and, provided you are using good, fresh fish, needs little messing around with to release its flavour. In the summer I might serve it with a salady salsa, and in the winter with a wholegrain mustard and lime sauce, or with vegetables and noodles for a heartier dish. The pan-fried salmon recipe in this chapter is perfect for a light lunch in summer with a girlfriend when you can sit in the garden and have a good gossip over a chilled glass of wine – or two.

I would also add that to get the best from fish you should always buy it as fresh as it can be. If you're not a great fish eater, make friends with your local fishmonger, or talk to someone on the fish counter at your local supermarket. You'll find that they will tell you which cuts are the best for what and which are the cheapest, and they'll always have some good suggestions on the best cooking method for each fish.

Smoked fish pâté

Scallops with parsley and lemon
vinaigrette

Fresh sardines warpped in vine leaves
with chilli and lemon butter

Tuna Niçoise with pan-fried quail eggs

Rosemary-infused monkfish

Grilled cod with home-made red pesto

Pan-fried salmon with chunky
guacamole

Tiger prawn stir-fry

Sea bass with vine tomatoes, olives
and capers

Smoked fish pâté

This tasty pâté is an appealing soft peachy-pink and packed with healthy fatty acids. Serve with toasted wholemeal pitta bread or toasted soda bread, sliced into fingers, for a light lunch. This tastes best if you make it with fishmonger kippers, but I have also made it using the supermarket boil-in-a-bag variety.

400g/14oz kipper fillets
25g/1oz melted unsalted butter
200g/7oz cream cheese
   (Philadelphia is best)
zest and juice of 1 lemon
1 garlic clove, peeled and
   crushed
3 tbsp extra virgin olive oil
black pepper
chopped chives to garnish

Prep time: 15 minutes
Cooking time: 4 minutes
(if using fishmonger kippers)

1 If using fishmonger kipper fillets, preheat the grill to high. Brush the fillets lightly with melted butter and grill, skin-side up, for 2 minutes. Flip them over and cook for a further 2 minutes. Leave to cool, then scrape off the skin and remove any large bones. If using boil-in-the-bag kippers, cook as instructed on the packet and then remove the skin.

2 Place the kippers, cream cheese, lemon zest and juice, garlic and pepper to taste in a food processor and blitz until smooth. With the motor still running, pour in the oil.

3 Spoon into a serving dish and chill. Sprinkle with chopped chives and serve with warmed wholemeal pitta bread.

Scallops with parsley and lemon vinaigrette

A really quick and easy starter, and one that never fails to impress. For my children it's also been a gentle introduction to something a little more sophisticated.

100ml/3^1/$_2$fl oz olive oil
20g pack of fresh flat-leaf
  parsley, roughly chopped
1 garlic clove, peeled and
  finely chopped
2 tbsp lemon zest
juice of 1 lemon
8 scallops, halved
salt and black pepper

Serves: 4
Prep time: 10 minutes
Cooking time: 5 minutes

1 Put all but 2 tablespoons of the oil into a frying pan and place over a low heat. Add the parsley, garlic and lemon zest and cook for 1 minute, letting it sizzle gently. Pour into a bowl and leave to cool.

2 Add the lemon juice, season with salt and pepper and whisk to combine.

3 Heat the remaining oil in another frying pan. Season the scallops on both sides and add to the frying pan. Fry over a medium-high heat for a minute or so to get a nice golden crust on the underside, then turn and cook for another 30 seconds, until golden on that side.

4 Place the scallops on serving plates and drizzle the parsley vinaigrette over and around them.

WHY NOT TRY...

Serve on a bed of wilted spinach leaves. Wilt them in the same pan you cook the scallops in to soak up the lemon juices.

Fresh sardines wrapped in vine leaves with chilli and lemon butter

This is a wonderful barbeque dish. Cooking the sardines in vine leaves protects them from any harsh heat and imbues them with a rich, smoky flavour. It is, of course, possible to cook them under a hot grill, if the weather is not up to a barbeque. If you can't get hold of vine leaves, use lightly oiled greaseproof paper and then wrap them up in tin foil.

50g/2oz softened butter
3 garlic cloves, peeled and
    crushed
2 large red chillies, deseeded
    and finely chopped
30g pack of fresh flat-leaf
    parsley, leaves finely
    chopped
zest of 1 lemon
12 fresh sardines
preserved vine leaves, rinsed
    and dried
olive oil for brushing
salt and black pepper
lemon wedges to serve

1 Get the barbecue going, or preheat the grill to hot.

2 Work together the softened butter, garlic, chillies, parsley and lemon zest. Season with salt and pepper. Rub the seasoned butter all over the inside and outside of the sardines.

3 Lightly brush the vine leaves with a little oil and then wrap each sardine in a vine leaf – I find that half a leaf is usually enough for each sardine.

4 Grill on the barbeque or under the grill for 2 minutes on each side. The vine leaves will be burnt and charred but the sardines will be cooked perfectly inside.

5 Serve with wedges of lemon and allow everyone to unwrap their sardines themselves.

Serves: 2-4
Prep time: 10 minutes
Cooking time: 4 minutes

Although the six of us love spending time together as a family, Gordon and I also believe in having individual time with each of the children. Of course, this is often easier said than done, so sometimes we just split up into two 'groups' and do different things. Both Jack and Matilda love watching and playing football, so this gives Gordon the perfect excuse to go to a game, with the added bonus of spending time with them; while I might play tennis with the other girls or take them swimming, or whatever else they fancy doing.

The holidays and weekends give us more time to spend in this way, but weekdays are always a bit of a challenge. It's not possible to plan any kind of set rota for having time with them, as we, and they, are so busy anyway, and unexpected activities often pop up on a weekly basis, making no two weeks the same. Often, by the time the children have got home and done everything they need to do of an evening, I can only snatch 15 minutes or so with each of them before they go to sleep. Even so, that's better than no time at all, and I love to sprawl over their beds and listen to them read, or just chat to them about school, friends and anything else they want to talk about. It's the perfect end to the day for them and me.

Tuna Niçoise with pan-fried quail eggs

This is a great Saturday lunch dish - it is a favourite that Gordon makes for the kids - they love the quail eggs, as the girls say they are like doll's eggs! To me a Niçoise has to be eaten at room temperature - none of the the ingredients should be fridge cold.

450g/1lb baby new potatoes, scrubbed
200g/7oz green beans
1 shallot, peeled
12-16 cherry tomatoes, cut in half around the middle
16 plump black olives, pitted
2 tbsp capers
16 marinated anchovies
2 Little Gem lettuce, cut into 1cm/^{1}/$_2$ inch shreds
1 handful of torn basil leaves
4 tuna loin steaks, each about 100g/3^1/$_2$oz
3 tbsp olive oil
1 tbsp balsamic vinegar
8 quail eggs
salt and black pepper

FOR THE VINAIGRETTE
1^1/$_2$ tbsp red wine vinegar
125ml/4fl oz extra virgin olive oil
125ml/4fl oz olive oil
1 tbsp groundnut oil
1 tbsp lemon juice

Serves: 4
Prep time: 40 minutes
Cooking time: 25 minutes

1 To make the vegetable salad, boil the potatoes for about 15 minutes until tender. Drain well, then halve. Trim the beans, then cook the beans in salted boiling water for 2 minutes. Drain and refresh in iced water - this will ensure they keep their lovely bright green colour instead of the slightly sludgy green look. Drain well once more and pat dry. Slice the shallot into rings. Mix the potatoes and beans with the shallot, tomatoes, olives, capers, anchovies, lettuce and basil.

2 Whisk together the vinaigrette ingredients and season with salt and pepper. Toss the vegetable salad in some of the vinaigrette and divide between four serving bowls.

3 Heat a large non-stick frying pan until really hot. Season the tuna steaks. Add 1 tablespoon of the oil, then arrange the tuna steaks in the pan. Cook them for 1-1^1/$_2$ minutes on each side until they feel lightly springy when pressed in the centre. The tuna is best when it is still pink in the middle.

4 Deglaze the pan with the balsamic vinegar, then turn the tuna steaks over so they are lightly coated in the vinegar. Add a little more seasoning, lift out the tuna and place a steak onto the salad in each serving bowl.

5 Heat another frying pan and add the remaining oil. Carefully break in the quail eggs and fry for about 30 seconds until they are just set, spooning over the oil as they cook. Season the eggs with salt and pepper, then add to each serving bowl. Drizzle over the remaining vinaigrette. Serve and enjoy!

Rosemary-infused monkfish

Monkfish needs strong flavours and in this recipe the rosemary and Parmesan give it a fresh flavour, ideal for eating outside in the summer. I specify ciabatta crumbs rather than normal white breadcrumbs, because they create much larger, coarser crumbs that crisp beautifully and help absorb the flavours.

1 × 800g/1lb 12oz monkfish
    tail, filleted
2 garlic cloves, peeled and
    crushed
4 sprigs of rosemary, leaves
    removed and finely chopped
juice of 1 lemon
4 tbsp olive oil
30g/1¼oz slice of ciabatta
    bread, processed into
    breadcrumbs
30g/1¼oz finely grated
    Parmesan cheese
salt and black pepper
lemon wedges to serve

Serves: 4
Prep time: 15 minutes plus
1-3 hours marinating
Cooking time: 30 minutes

1 Cut the monkfish into eight even-sized pieces. Combine the garlic, rosemary, lemon juice, oil and pepper to taste in a medium-sized bowl, just large enough to fit the fish. Add the fish to the marinade and, using your hands, turn the fish in the marinade to make sure that it is thoroughly coated. Leave for 1–3 hours, during which time occasionally move the fish around so that the bits poking out at the top get a chance to absorb the flavours.

2 Preheat the oven to 200°C/400°F/GM6.

3 Find a roasting tin that fits the fish fairly tightly. Arrange the fish in it evenly, sprinkle with salt and pour over the remaining marinade. Sprinkle the breadcrumbs and Parmesan over the top of the fish, then pop the tin in the oven.

4 Cook for 30 minutes or until the fish is cooked through and the topping is lightly browned. Serve with some of the juices spooned over, and with lemon wedges.

WHY NOT TRY...

Serve with steamed rice and fresh peas, flageolet beans, red onion and mint salad on page 152.

Grilled cod with home-made red pesto

Cod really does taste better the fresher it is. The intense flavour of this pesto complements the smooth, creamy flavour of the cod perfectly. I love pesto, which is why this recipe makes so much. If you prefer, you can put some aside rather than serve it all with the cod.

50g/2oz butter, melted, plus
　　extra for greasing
4 × 200g/7oz pieces of thick,
　　unskinned cod fillet
salt and black pepper

FOR THE PESTO
2 red peppers, quartered,
　　deseeded and all white pith
　　removed
1 large red chilli, deseeded
150g/5oz sun-dried tomatoes
50g/2oz pitted black olives
1 tbsp extra virgin olive oil
1 garlic clove, peeled
1 tbsp oregano leaves

Serves: 4
Prep time: 25 minutes
Cooking time: 10 minutes
plus roasting the peppers

1　Preheat the grill to high.

2　Start by making the red pesto. Arrange the peppers and chilli, skin-side up, on a baking sheet and put under the grill for 10–15 minutes, until the skins are charred and bubbling. Remove from the grill and immediately place in a freezer bag or plastic food container with an airtight lid. Seal and allow to cool until easy to handle. You will now find that the skins slip off easily.

3　Place the skinned peppers and chilli in a food processor with the sun-dried tomatoes, olives, olive oil, garlic and oregano. Blitz to a smooth paste and check the seasoning.

4　If you have made the pesto in advance, reheat the grill to hot. Use either a greased baking tray or a non-stick tray. Brush the cod with melted butter and season on both sides with salt and pepper. Arrange the fish, skin-side up, on the tray and place under the grill. Cook for 10 minutes or until the skin is crisp and the fish is cooked through.

5　Divide the pesto between four warm plates and carefully arrange the cod on top. Serve immediately.

WHY NOT TRY...

Serve with crushed new potatoes and a seasonal salad.

I love eating fish because I like its texture and flavour, but I also think it is a really important part of my family's diet because it's such a healthy food choice, so I do try to serve it up once or twice a week.

The supermarket shelves are now packed with products that contain added omega-3 fatty acids – eggs, fruit juices, bread, margarine and children's drinks – but one food that naturally contains this fatty acid is oily fish. So I like to cook oily fish – such as tuna, mackerel, salmon or sardines – twice a week, if not more, because they're real superfoods. The reason everyone is talking about omega-3 is because research has shown it has anti-inflammatory properties (which are good for joints and aches and pains) and also that if eaten regularly it can help reduce the risk of heart disease.

We've always talked to the children about the importance of nutrition and knowing where their food comes from, but after my mother-in-law had a heart by-pass, there was another conversation about the need to keep their hearts healthy through diet and exercise, and they've happily added eating oily fish to their already active lifestyle.

There are also claims that omega-3 acids can help the development of brain tissue, but that's still being debated, so at the moment getting their two portions of oily fish a week is not a good enough reason for them not to do their homework!

Pan-fried salmon with chunky guacamole

This is quite a summery dish, perfect for a light lunch in the garden with a chilled glass of wine. Choose avocados that are nice and ripe – the skin should easily dent when you push it.

2 tbsp olive oil
4 salmon fillets, each about
    100g/3^1/$_2$oz
salt and black pepper

FOR THE GUACAMOLE
2 ripe avocados, stone
    removed and cut into small
    dice
juice of 1 lime
^{1}/$_4$ red onion, peeled and
    finely chopped
1 small red chili, deseeded
    and diced
2 tbsp finely chopped fresh
    coriander
2 tbsp soured cream

1 Start by making the guacamole. Put the diced avocado into a mixing bowl and squeeze over the lime juice. Add the onion, chilli, coriander and soured cream and stir through. Add a pinch of salt and a grinding of pepper and put to one side while you cook the salmon.

2 Heat a non-stick frying pan until hot and add the oil. Fry the salmon, skin-side down, for 3 minutes. Flip over and cook the other side for about 2 minutes. The flesh should be slightly springy when pressed. Season the salmon lightly with salt and pepper.

3 Spoon the guacamole onto the centre of each plate, being generous. Place a salmon fillet on top of the guacamole and serve.

Serves: 4
Prep time: 20 minutes
Cooking time: 5-7 minutes

WHY NOT TRY...

Delicious served with a drizzle of reduced balsamic vinegar over the top.

Tiger prawn stir-fry

A very simple and tasty dish – the vegetables add a great variety of colour and the prawns and noodles make this a healthy, nutritious, quick and easy meal.

125g/4oz medium egg noodles
2 tbsp sunflower oil
1 garlic clove, peeled and thinly sliced
1 red chilli, deseeded and thinly sliced
1 carrot, peeled and cut into very thin strips
125g/4oz tenderstem broccoli
4 spring onions, trimmed and cut into strips
1 red pepper, deseeded and thinly sliced
200g/7oz raw tiger prawns
1 tbsp toasted sesame oil
2 tbsp soy sauce
2 tbsp rice vinegar
1 handful of fresh coriander, finely chopped, plus extra to serve
4 tbsp unsalted cashew nuts

Serves: 2
Prep time: 25 minutes
Cooking time: 15 minutes

1 Cook the noodles as instructed on the packet, drain and rinse quickly under cold water to separate. Drain again.

2 Heat the sunflower oil in a wok or large frying pan and lightly fry the garlic and chilli for about 1 minute. Add the carrot, broccoli, spring onions and red pepper and cook, stirring constantly, for 3–4 minutes. Add the prawns and cook until they turn pink. Add the sesame oil, soy sauce and rice vinegar and sprinkle in three-quarters of the coriander. Add the noodles to the pan along with the cashew nuts. Heat all together thoroughly. Add a little more soy sauce if desired and make sure the prawns and vegetables are evenly stirred through the noodles.

3 Serve straight away with a little more coriander on the top of each portion.

Sea bass with vine tomatoes, olives and capers

This is a wonderful summer fish dish that can be served with traditional dauphinoise potatoes (see page 184) or crushed new potatoes. Alternatively, try with boiled Camargue rice tossed in a lemony dressing.

300g/11oz vine-ripened cherry tomatoes
100g/3½oz pitted black olives
2 tbsp capers, rinsed
4 tbsp olive oil plus a little more for drizzling
1 sea bass, weighing about 800g/1lb 12oz, filleted, skin left on
2 tbsp dry vermouth (Noilly Prat is best)
2 tbsp finely chopped fresh flat-leaf parsley
salt and black pepper

Serves: 4
Prep time: 10 minutes
Cooking time: 15 minutes

1 Preheat the oven to 180°C/350°F/GM4.

2 Keeping the tomatoes attached to the vine, cut the vine so that you have small bunches of about 4 tomatoes. Place the tomatoes, olives and capers in a roasting tin with the oil and carefully toss around making sure everything is coated in oil. Season with a good grinding of pepper.

3 Lay the sea bass on top of the tomatoes, season with salt and pepper and drizzle with a little more oil. Place in the oven for 15 minutes. Halfway through the cooking time, add the Noilly Prat and baste the fillets with the cooking juices.

4 When the fish is cooked, transfer it to two warm plates. Carefully take out the tomatoes, trying to keep them attached to the vine, and arrange beside the fish. Throw the parsley into the roasting tin and stir into the capers, olives and cooking juices. Spoon the mixture over the fish fillets and serve immediately.

WHY NOT TRY...

If you have trouble getting hold of a large sea bass, simply use four ordinary sea bass fillets.

Simply
LAMB

There's always a constant stream of people coming through our house, day in, day out. It might be film crews, photographers, journalists, or friends or family, but there's always something going on.

In addition to all this, the children often have friends over for tea after school or sport, and some weekends bring visits from family or friends. When we have people over I don't want to be stuck in the kitchen while they all relax and catch up amongst themselves, and so this is where one-pot dishes are brilliant. Whether it's a deliciously fruity bobotie, a curry, or a simple roast, being able to shove it all into one pot and let it do its thing while I do mine is great.

If there's one roast that's hands-down favourite in our house, though, it's roast lamb. We don't just keep it for Sunday best; we'll quite often eat it during the week, too (if all the children are home early with no stragglers coming in later). But it's also a hit with friends and family as a lovely languorous Sunday lunch, when we can sit around and chat and put off thinking about the next manic week ahead for a few more hours.

Balsamic lamb salad

Bobotie

Rack of lamb with olive tapenade crust

Irish lamb stew with dumplings

Leg of lamb with pancetta, rosemary
  and tomato sauce

Sticky hoisin lamb

Lamb rogan josh

Lamb kofta

Fruity lamb shanks

Balsamic lamb salad

This is an easy after-work supper dish. It won't take long and all the ingredients can be very quickly picked up from a supermarket without any hassle.

600g/1lb 5oz boneless loin of lamb, skinned and fat removed
500g/1lb 2oz baby new potatoes
4 tbsp olive oil
2 tsp coriander seeds, lightly crushed in a pestle and mortar
salt and black pepper
100g bag of mixed wild rocket and chard leaves

FOR THE MARINADE
2 tbsp olive oil
150ml/5fl oz balsamic vinegar
150ml/5fl oz red wine
5 plump garlic cloves, peeled and lightly crushed
5 sprigs of rosemary

Serves: 4
Prep time: 5 minutes plus marinating
Cooking time: 35 minutes

1 As soon as you get home, mix together the marinade ingredients, then dunk in the lamb and leave for as long as you can. Preheat the oven to 190°C/375°F/GM5.

2 Put the potatoes into a pan, cover with water and add a good pinch of salt. Bring to the boil, then reduce the heat and simmer for 2 minutes. Drain the potatoes and return them to the pan to allow the excess water to steam away in the residual heat of the pan.

3 Add 3 tablespoons of the oil, the crushed coriander seeds and some salt and pepper to the potatoes and turn to coat them with the oily mixture. Transfer to a baking tray, place in the oven and bake for 25–30 minutes, turning them halfway through, until the potatoes are golden and soft in the middle.

4 Meanwhile, heat the remaining oil in an ovenproof frying pan on a medium-high heat. Take the lamb out of the marinade and drain well. Reserve the marinade. Cook the lamb in the frying pan for about 5 minutes on each side, until well browned. The lamb should be only slightly pink in the centre. Take out of the pan and set aside on a warm plate.

5 Remove the garlic cloves from the marinade and pour about half into the frying pan. Bring to the boil and reduce by about a quarter.

6 Cut the lamb into thin slices, about 5mm/$^1/_4$ inch wide. Arrange the salad leaves and the potatoes – oil, coriander seeds and all – on four large plates. Pop the sliced lamb on top and drizzle over a little of the reduced hot marinade.

Bobotie

This is a South African dish, which I have adapted. It is absolutely delicious and my South African brother-in-law, Jonty loves it. I think of it as a lighter version of shepherd's pie.

1 medium slice of bread plus
   full-fat milk to soak
25g/1oz butter
2 medium onions
2 garlic cloves
2cm/$^3/_4$ inch fresh ginger
2 tsp garam masala
$^1/_2$ tsp ground turmeric
1 tsp ground cumin
1 tsp ground coriander
2 cloves
2 tsp ground allspice
1 tsp dried herbs
500g/1lb 2oz minced lamb
1$^1/_2$ tbsp malt vinegar
50g/2oz dried apricots
50g/2oz sultanas
25g/1oz flaked almonds
3 tbsp mango chutney
4 tbsp chopped parsley
2 bay leaves

FOR THE TOPPING
250ml/9fl oz full-fat milk
3 large eggs
4 thin slices of lemon
2 bay leaves

1 Preheat the oven to 180°C/350°F/GM4.

2 Soak the bread in just enough milk to cover, then mash with a fork. Put to one side.

3 Peel and finely chop the onions and garlic. Peel and grate the ginger. Melt the butter in a large saucepan over a low-medium heat and cook the onions and garlic for 5–7 minutes, until softened. Stir in the ginger, garam masala, turmeric, cumin, coriander, cloves, allspice and herbs and cook for 1–2 minutes.

4 In a separate pan, fry the lamb mince on a medium heat until coloured, breaking up any lumps. Drain off the excess fat and add to the onion mixture with the mashed bread and the malt vinegar. Heat this all together, mixing well.

5 Chop the apricots, then stir them in with the sultanas, flaked almonds, mango chutney, parsley and bay leaves.

6 Tip the mixture into an medium-sized ovenproof dish, press it down firmly, then set aside while you make the topping.

7 Beat the milk and eggs together, season with salt and pepper and pour over the top of the mince. Put the lemon slices and bay leaves on the top. Place in the oven and cook for 30–35 minutes until the top has set and is golden.

Serves: 4
Prep time: 35 minutes
Cooking time: 40–45 minutes

Rack of lamb with olive tapenade crust

This takes minutes to put together and tastes wonderful. Serve with a flavoured mashed potato in the winter, or dauphinoise potatoes (see page 184) when the sun shines.

1 × 7-cutlet rack of lamb
1 tbsp Dijon mustard
good-quality olive oil to serve

FOR THE TAPENADE
1 slice of ciabatta bread,
    weighing about 15g/$^1/_2$oz
25g/1oz pitted black olives
25g/1oz pitted green olives
zest of 1 lemon
1 anchovy fillet
1 plump garlic clove, peeled
2 tbsp extra virgin olive oil
1 tbsp red wine vinegar
black pepper

Serves: 2
Prep time: 15 minutes
Cooking time: 25 minutes
plus resting

1 Preheat the oven to 220°C/425°F/GM7.

2 Put the ciabatta in a food processor and pulse until you have fairly coarse crumbs. Tip the breadcrumbs into a mixing bowl.

3 Put the remaining tapenade ingredients into the bowl of the food processor and blitz until well chopped. Mix together with the breadcrumbs.

4 Put the rack of lamb into a small roasting tin, fat side up, and brush the top with the mustard. Press the breadcrumb mixture over the fat. The meat should be cooked crumb side uppermost.

5 Cook for 25 minutes, then remove from the oven and leave to rest in a warm place for about 10 minutes. The meat should be pink and slightly undercooked. Serve with the cooking juices from the pan poured on top and a little drizzle of oil.

Irish lamb stew with dumplings

This dish has been made by busy people for generations. Traditionally, you wouldn't make it with barley or dumplings but, quite simply, this is how I like it best. In return for 15 minutes of vegetable peeling and chopping, you have a delicious and very healthy meal for very little effort. Serve with plain boiled Savoy cabbage.

1.25kg/2³/₄lb lamb neck fillet, sliced into 2.5cm/1 inch pieces
4 tbsp plain flour, seasoned with salt and pepper
2 onions, peeled and thinly sliced
2 sticks of celery, finely sliced
3 large carrots, peeled and cut diagonally into chunks
2 large leeks, cleaned, trimmed and cut diagonally into chunks
4 medium floury potatoes, peeled and quartered
3 tbsp pearl barley
1.5 litres/2¹/₂ pints boiling water
2 bay leaves
salt and black pepper

FOR THE DUMPLINGS
175g/6oz self-raising flour
75g/3oz suet
3 tbsp finely chopped fresh flat-leaf parsley
125ml/4fl oz water

Serves: 6
Prep time: 40 minutes
Cooking time: 2¹/₄ hours

1 Preheat the oven to 160°C/325°F/GM3.

2 Dry the pieces of lamb on absorbent kitchen paper, if necessary. Spread the seasoned flour out on a plate, then roll the meat in the flour, shaking off any excess. Layer the meat and vegetables in a large heavy-based casserole dish with a tight-fitting lid, seasoning well with salt and pepper between the layers. Sprinkle the pearl barley over the top and season again with salt and pepper. Pour the boiling water over and pop in the bay leaves. Put the lid on the casserole and cook in the oven for 1³/₄ hours.

3 About 15 minutes before the end of the cooking time, increase the oven temperature to 200°C/400°F/GM6 and make the dumplings. Combine the flour, suet and parsley in a bowl and season well with salt and pepper. Then, carefully add enough of the water to form a fairly stiff, elastic paste – you may need a little more. Knead lightly for a few seconds, until smooth, then divide into 12 pieces and shape into balls.

4 Remove the casserole from the oven. Check the seasoning and add more salt and pepper, if necessary. Dot the dumpling mixture over the top of the stew. Return the casserole to the oven and cook, uncovered, for a further 30 minutes until the dumplings are crusty and golden.

Leg of lamb with pancetta, rosemary and tomato sauce

Mum always used to make this – it was one of her classic Sunday lunches. Just the smell of this aromatic dish takes me right back to my childhood, and the kids love it. Use any leftovers for the rogan josh on page 115.

2.5kg/5^1/$_2$lb leg of lamb
olive oil
3 garlic cloves, peeled and
    finely sliced
small sprigs of rosemary
salt and black pepper

FOR THE SAUCE
200g/7oz cubed pancetta
1 medium red onion, peeled
    and finely chopped
1 garlic clove, peeled and
    finely chopped
200ml/7fl oz dry/medium
    white wine
2 tbsp fresh rosemary leaves,
    finely chopped
2 × 400g tins of chopped
    tomatoes

Serves: 6
Prep time: 30 minutes
Cooking time: 2 hours
plus resting

1 Preheat the oven to 220°C/425°F/GM7.

2 Place the lamb in a large roasting tin. Blot the skin with absorbent kitchen paper, brush lightly all over with oil and rub salt and pepper into the skin. Using a sharp knife, cut little pockets in the skin of the leg and slip in slivers of garlic and small sprigs of rosemary.

3 Put the lamb into the oven for 20 minutes to sear the meat. Take the lamb out of the oven, then turn the oven down to 190°C/375°F/GM5 – leaving the door open will speed the process. Put the lamb back into the oven and cook for about 1^1/$_2$ hours, basting from time to time.

4 Meanwhile, make your sauce. Add the pancetta to a hot frying pan and fry until crisp, then reduce the heat, add the onion and garlic and cook until soft. Pour in the wine and simmer until reduced by about two-thirds. Add the rosemary and tomatoes, season with salt and pepper and bring to a simmer. Cook over a low heat for 20 minutes.

5 When the lamb has been in the oven for about 1 hour, remove the tin and pour the sauce over the meat. Return to the oven for the remaining 30 minutes.

6 Remove from the oven and leave the lamb to rest for at least 10 minutes before serving.

Sticky hoisin lamb

A delicious sticky mess! It is really tricky to find a good recipe for home-made hoisin – there are so many different versions and indeed arguments about it, so I just buy mine.

3 tbsp hoisin sauce (either home-made or shop bought)

2 tbsp soy sauce

1 tsp sesame oil

1 tbsp rice wine

1/2 tsp five-spice powder

400g/14oz boneless loin of lamb

250g/9oz green beans, trimmed

1 red chilli, deseeded and cut into thin strips

2 tbsp finely chopped fresh coriander

1/4 cucumber, cut into dice

4 spring onions, cut into thin strips

2 tsp olive oil

juice of 1/2 lime

2 tsp sesame seeds, lightly toasted in a dry frying pan

salt and black pepper

Serves: 2
Prep time: 15 minutes plus marinating for 1 hour
Cooking time: 15 minutes

1 Spoon the hoisin sauce into a flat dish along with the soy sauce, sesame oil, rice wine and five-spice and stir to combine. Put in the lamb and turn to coat evenly in the mixture. Leave to marinate for an hour or so, turning regularly.

2 Meanwhile, heat a pan of water with 1 teaspoon of salt until simmering. Add the green beans and cook until they are tender but still with a little crunch – 4–5 minutes. Tip them into a sieve and put to one side.

3 Put a griddle pan on the hob and heat until hot. Take the lamb out of the marinade and grill for about 5 minutes, turning once, until nicely seared on both sides. Reduce the heat and continue cooking for 5 minutes, until the lamb is pink on the inside and slightly scorched outside, but not burnt, just a really nice colour. Transfer to a plate and leave to rest for 5 minutes while you prepare the salad.

4 Place the green beans along with the chilli, coriander, cucumber and spring onions in a mixing bowl and add the olive oil, lime juice, salt and pepper. Carefully toss through so the dressing coats everything evenly. Arrange the salad in a serving dish.

5 Transfer the lamb to a board, then carefully slice and arrange on top of the salad. Sprinkle over the sesame seeds and serve.

Lamb rogan josh

There are always leftovers from a leg of lamb in our house – unless we have had surprise guests! This untraditional rogan josh is made from leftovers of the leg of lamb recipe on page 111. I also include all the bits of sauce and trimmings from around the roasting tray.

2 tbsp groundnut oil

2 medium onions, peeled and finely chopped

2 garlic cloves, peeled and finely chopped

2 tsp salt

1 red chilli, deseeded and finely chopped

2 tsp curry powder

1 tsp ground turmeric

3 tsp garam masala

2 tsp ground coriander

2 tsp ground cumin

about 500g/1lb 2oz leftover cooked leg of lamb (see page 111), diced into bite-sized pieces (include any sauce)

about 300g/11oz tinned chopped tomatoes

4 tbsp natural yoghurt

2–3 tbsp hot and spicy mango chutney

4 tbsp chopped fresh coriander

basmati rice to serve

2 tbsp lightly toasted flaked almonds to garnish

1 Heat the oil in a large pan on a low-medium heat, add the onions, garlic, salt and red chilli and cook until softened. Add the curry powder to taste, turmeric, garam masala, ground coriander and cumin and stir with the onions to form a paste. Add the lamb and any sauce and stir to mix thoroughly.

2 Add the tomatoes (adjust quantity as necessary depending on the amount of leftover sauce from the lamb – you may need more or less) and yoghurt and simmer gently for 8–10 minutes, until the lamb is thoroughly heated through. Stir in the chutney, adjusting to taste. Add 3 tablespoons of the fresh coriander, reserving a little to sprinkle on the top.

3 Serve the lamb on a bed of rice with the coriander sprinkled over the top, and scattered with the almonds.

WHY NOT TRY...

It is difficult to give exact quantities for this recipe as it really is a matter of taste – no two curries are ever the same, so adjust the yoghurt/ chutney as you feel necessary, or add a little more salt.

Serves: 4
Prep time: 30 minutes
Cooking time: 20 minutes

Lamb kofta

This just couldn't be easier. The secret is owning a food processor! The kofta can be cooked either under a hot grill, or, weather permitting, on the barbeque.

2 medium onions, peeled
   and cut into quarters
1 tsp ground cumin
1 tsp ground coriander
500g/1lb 2oz minced lamb
20g pack of fresh flat-leaf
   parsley, leaves only
1 egg
2 tbsp fresh mint
100g/3^1/$_2$oz sultanas
salt and black pepper

FOR THE SAUCE
400g/14oz plain yoghurt
1 medium onion, peeled and
   grated using a microplane
   grater
2 tbsp chopped fresh dill

Serves: 4
Prep time: 25 minutes plus
30 minutes soaking the skewers
Cooking time: about
15 minutes

1 Start by soaking 16 × 30.5cm/12 inch wooden skewers in cold water for 30 minutes. Preheat the grill, or fire up the barbecue.

2 Put the onions, cumin and coriander in a food processor and blitz to a pulp. Add the lamb, parsley, mint and egg and pulse until the mixture is bound together. Tip the meat mixture into a mixing bowl and stir in the sultanas. Season well with salt and pepper.

3 Wet your hands well, then take about 1 rounded tablespoon of the mixture in your hands and mould into a sausage shape. Push a skewer into the sausage and squeeze the meat around it. The kofta should be about two-thirds the length of the skewer. Make all 16 skewers in the same way.

4 Line the grill pan with a sheet of foil, place the kofta on it and cook under the hot grill for 10–15 minutes until cooked through. Or cook on the barbecue for about 10 minutes.

5 While the meat is cooking, make the sauce. Mix the yoghurt with the grated onion and dill. Season with salt and pepper.

6 Serve the kofta immediately accompanied by the sauce and a crisp salad.

Sunday night always comes round too quickly for our liking, and we can't ignore the fact that it means the weekend is now over. In our house, Sunday night is very much like a weeknight, which means getting ready for school the next day.

With four children who have school and activities going on every day, it's hard to keep track of what they need and when – especially because it seems to change every term. I haven't got time to get everything together for each of them every morning, as it's hard enough trying to make breakfast and race out of the door to school and work, so I've handed that job back to them. To make it easier, we have charts outside their rooms and downstairs that show every day of the week and whether they need football kit, tennis gear, swimming stuff, or art overalls. Each night they have to lay out their uniforms, pack their bags with whatever they need for the next day, and make up their snackbox and drink and put them in the fridge. Next morning, it's up to them to remember to take everything with them – if they forget, I won't take it in to them, and they're unlikely to forget again!

I've always tried to encourage the children to do things for themselves and to take responsibility, which is why we expect the kids to muck in around the house. It's nothing too heavy, just the usual stuff like making their beds, keeping their rooms tidy, emptying the dishwasher and getting together everything they need to take with them when they leave the house. If we all have our own jobs and do them, it means things get done much quicker, giving us all more family time.

Fruity lamb shanks

This is a delicious dish inspired by traditional slow-cooked Moroccan dishes. Ras el hanout is a blend of Moroccan spices now widely available in supermarkets. Lamb shanks are now also easily available from supermarket meat counters, but if you find yourself in a butcher's, ask for mutton shanks instead, as they have a fantastic depth of flavour and the added advantage of supporting British sheep farmers trying to sell their sheep aged over 24 months.

4 lamb or mutton shanks
2 tbsp olive oil
4 tsp ras el hanout
400g tin of chopped tomatoes
600ml/1 pint water
1 large carrot, halved
   lengthways and cut
   into thick batons
215g tin of pitted prunes in
   fruit juice (not syrup), juice
   reserved
150g/5oz dried apricots
2 bay leaves
400g tin of chickpeas, drained
   through a sieve and then
   rinsed
75g/3oz blanched almonds
40g pack of fresh coriander,
   leaves and stalks separated
   (reserve the stalks for paste)
plain yoghurt, to serve
salt and black pepper

1 Preheat the oven to 170°C/325°F/GM3.

2 Put all the paste ingredients into the bowl of a food processor with the coriander stalks and blitz until the paste is smooth.

3 Dry the lamb or mutton shanks with absorbent kitchen paper. Warm the oil in a large, heavy-based casserole dish with a tight-fitting lid on a medium heat and, as it begins to shimmer, add the shanks. Brown on all sides, then remove from the casserole and put to one side.

4 Reduce the heat, then add the paste and ras el hanout to the oil. Cook for about 3 minutes until the smells waft up from the pan.

5 Return the shanks to the pan and pour in the tomatoes and water. Add the carrot, prunes and apricots and 2 tablespoons of the prune juice. Pop in the bay leaves and season well with salt and pepper. Put the lid on the casserole and cook in the oven for 1 1/2 hours. Add the chickpeas and return to the oven for a further 45 minutes.

6 Meanwhile, toast the almonds in a dry frying pan on a medium heat until they are golden brown, then put to one side.

7 About 10 minutes before you are ready to eat, prepare the couscous. It couldn't be easier. Put the couscous, salt and butter in a heatproof bowl. Pour the boiling water over, cover with a clean tea towel and leave to soak for 5 minutes. Just before you are ready to serve, add the lemon zest and fluff up the grains with a fork.

FOR THE PASTE

2 medium onions, peeled
   and roughly chopped
5 garlic cloves, peeled
1 red chilli, deseeded and
   chopped
1 stick of celery, roughly
   chopped
5cm/2 inch piece of fresh root
   ginger, peeled and chopped
1 small handful of fresh
   coriander leaves

FOR THE COUSCOUS

450g/1lb couscous
$^1/_2$ tsp salt
25g/1oz butter
450ml/15fl oz boiling water
finely grated zest of 1 lemon

Serves: 4
Prep time: 40 minutes
Cooking time: 2$^1/_4$ hours

WHY NOT TRY...

**If you cannot find ras el
hanout, use $^1/_4$ tsp each of
ground coriander, cumin
and chilli powder instead.**

8 When the time is up, the lamb should be soft and
   falling off the bone. Sprinkle the coriander leaves and
   toasted almonds over the meat. Serve in warm shallow
   bowls with lots of couscous and a bowl of yoghurt for
   people to help themselves to.

Simply
PORK

I grew up on a farm that kept quite a lot of livestock, including pigs. We ate a great deal of pork, because it was always on hand, and so this meat has always been part of my diet. Pork, in some form or another, features quite often in my weekly menu, probably because of my childhood memories of my mother cooking it at home, but also because it's so versatile. From the comfort of a bacon sarnie to a more sophisticated meal like the pork en papillotte in this chapter, you can always find some way of cooking pork that suits your mood or the occasion.

I'm never without bacon or pancetta in the fridge – they're perfect for a quick pasta and sauce, or tossed in a salad – and sausages and pork chops are the most convenient fast food for hungry homecoming children. There's bound to be one cut of pork that will appeal, and a method to suit, whether roasted, pan-fried, grilled, or barbecued.

My all-time favourite indulgence is maple bacon; there's something about its sweet flavour and it makes an ordinary meal something special. Although I like the children to have a good healthy breakfast before they go to school, weekends are all about relaxing the rules a little and treating yourself, and the one thing that's guaranteed to get the kids out of their beds and downstairs to breakfast is the smell of grilling bacon wafting through the house. And, it has to be said, an egg and bacon sarnie is the ultimate hangover food to get the adults back on track after a late night!

Figs wrapped in prosciutto

Bacon, egg, avocado and Little Gem salad

Ham and asparagus toast

Ham spinach and Gruyère croissant ring

Savoy cabbage, apple and pork chop
  en papillote

Cauliflower cheese and bacon quiche

Herb-crusted pork fillet with creamed leeks

Roast pork loin with cannellini beans,
  pancetta and thyme

Chorizo sausage tortilla with
  grilled pepper salad

Pork escalopes with spicy prune chutney

Sausages with apples and juniper berries

Figs wrapped in prosciutto

This is a simple and effective starter, or mix with salad leaves for a more substantial lunch dish. Fresh ripe figs complemented by the prosciutto are just delicious.

6 fresh figs
6 slices prosciutto ham
150g/5oz ripe Taleggio cheese
1 knob of butter
extra virgin olive oil and good-
   quality balsamic vinegar
   to drizzle
rocket leaves to serve
   (optional)

Serves: 3 as a salad
Prep time: 15 minutes
Cooking time: 15 minutes

1 Preheat the grill and slice off the very tops of the figs.

2 Wrap the prosciutto around the sides of the figs, then place 1 teaspoon of the cheese onto the sliced surface of the figs.

3 Heat the butter in an ovenproof pan, then sit the figs in the pan to warm the bases. Place under the grill to melt the cheese until it is bubbling and going slightly golden.

4 Put onto your serving plate and lightly drizzle over with the oil followed by balsamic vinegar. Serve immediately. Delicious served on a bed of rocket leaves.

Bacon, egg, avocado and Little Gem salad

A classic combination that needs little added.

2 Little Gem lettuces
2 eggs
6 rashers of unsmoked back
  bacon
1 ripe avocado
$1/2$ lemon, juiced
2 tsp chopped fresh chives
salt

FOR THE DRESSING
2 tbsp olive oil
1 tbsp white wine vinegar
1 tsp grain mustard
black pepper

Serves: 2
Prep time: 15 minutes
Cooking time: 10 minutes

1 Cut the stems off the lettuces, separate the leaves and rinse, then leave to drain on the side.

2 Meanwhile, bring a pan of water to the boil, add the eggs and boil for 5 minutes exactly – they should then be cooked but with a lovely runny yolk. As soon as you have timed 5 minutes, put them under cold water to instantly cool them. As soon as they are cool enough to handle, peel them carefully and put to one side.

3 Lay the bacon in a cold dry pan. Put the pan on the heat and cook the bacon until lightly crispy and slightly golden. Drain the bacon on absorbent kitchen paper.

4 Halve the avocado and remove the stone and outer skin. Slice into fairly thin slices, then squeeze the lemon juice over them.

5 Divide the lettuce between two serving plates, add 3 bacon rashers to each plate followed by slices of avocado.

6 Cut the eggs into quarters lengthways over the salad so that any runny yolk spills onto the salad. Sprinkle over a little salt.

7 To make the dressing, mix the oil with the vinegar and mustard and add a grinding of black pepper. Whisk together and dress the salad just before serving. Finish off with a sprinkling of chives and serve.

Ham and asparagus toast

A really simple supper with great effect.

12 asparagus spears
drizzle of olive oil
2 large slices of crusty white
    bread (farmhouse loaf or
    something similar)
2 tbsp mayonnaise
2 tsp grain mustard
4 slices of honey-roast ham,
    cut into rough strips
50g/2oz mix of Parmesan and
    Gruyère cheese, finely grated
salt and black pepper

Serves: 2
Prep time: 10 minutes
Cooking time: 10-15 minutes

1 Preheat the grill.

2 Steam or blanch the asparagus, whichever method
   you prefer, for 2-3 minutes, but leave them slightly
   undercooked. Transfer them to a shallow mixing bowl,
   drizzle with a little oil, sprinkle with salt and pepper
   and leave for a moment.

3 Meanwhile, toast the white bread on both sides. Mix
   the mayonnaise with the mustard and spread onto the
   crusty toast. Layer the ham onto both slices.

4 Lay 6 asparagus spears on each slice, then sprinkle
   over the cheese. Place this under the grill for 5-10
   minutes until the cheese is bubbling and slightly
   browning. Serve while hot.

Ham, spinach and Gruyère croissant ring

I once saw a version of this at a demonstration I went to and thought it a great idea. This is my version but adapt as you wish. Ideally, cook this on a pizza stone.

oil for greasing
2 × 240g packs of croissant
   dough
250g/9oz spinach, washed
10 slices of honey-roast ham,
   cut into strips
zest of 1 lemon
10 cherry tomatoes, halved
5 spring onions, chopped into
   rings about 5mm/¼ inch
   thick
10 small button mushrooms,
   sliced into quarters
50g/2oz rocket leaves
5 tbsp mascarpone cheese
50g/2oz Gruyère cheese,
   finely grated
black pepper

Serves: 4
Prep time: 20 minutes
Cooking time: 30 minutes

1 Preheat the oven to 180°C/350°F/GM4. Oil a pizza stone or grease a baking tray. Leave the croissant dough in the fridge until the last minute.

2 Start by blanching the spinach. Bring a pan of water to the boil, drop in the spinach and allow it to wilt for 3 minutes. Remove from the pan and leave to drain over the pan – this takes a little while but you don't want excess water in the dough ring.

3 Meanwhile, put the ham into a large mixing bowl, add the lemon zest, tomatoes, spring onions, mushrooms and rocket. Once the spinach has drained, stir the mascarpone cheese through it and add to the ham mix in the bowl. Add a good grinding of black pepper.

4 Take the dough out of the fridge, lay it out on a chopping board and separate along the perforations until you have squares. Cut each square diagonally so that you then have triangles. Arrange the triangles so they overlap and are in a large circle – the idea being you place your filling along the middle then pull over the top tips of the triangle and tuck underneath to encase the filling. Continue until you have used all your triangles, then spoon on the filling. Finish by sprinkling the Gruyère cheese over the filling, then fold the triangle tips over and tuck them underneath.

5 Place in the oven and cook for 30 minutes. Ensure the dough is cooked through and has a golden top. Serve immediately.

Savoy cabbage, apple and pork chop en papillote

Quick, easy and healthy.

2 tsp olive oil plus extra for
  brushing
2 pork chops, trimmed
50g/2oz butter
1/2 Savoy cabbage, very finely
  shredded
1 banana shallot, peeled
  and sliced
2 Cox's apples, cored and
  coarsely grated
squeeze of lemon juice
1 tsp sesame oil
15g pack of fresh thyme,
  chopped
salt and black pepper

Serves: 2
Prep time: 15 minutes
Cooking time: 25 minutes

1 Preheat the oven to 200°C/400°F/GM6. You will need 2 squares of parchment paper, each large enough to hold a pork chop and accompaniments, and to then seal.

2 Start by heating the olive oil in a pan large enough to hold both the pork chops. Season the chops, then sear them for 1–2 minutes on each side, until well browned. Add the butter to the pan and swirl it around as it melts, to colour the chops, then turn them over again. Take off the heat.

3 Mix the cabbage with the shallot and apple in a mixing bowl, season with salt and pepper, then add a squeeze of lemon juice.

4 Lightly brush both parchment paper squares with oil. Divide the cabbage, shallot and apple mix onto the centre of each square. Drizzle over 1/2 tsp of sesame oil to each. Place a pork chop onto each mound, divide the thyme and sprinkle over the top. Add a grinding of pepper and a pinch of salt. Encase the ingredients within the parchment paper, fold over the top and tuck down into a neat package. Place the packages onto an oven tray and bake in the oven for about 15 minutes until tender and cooked through.

5 Unwrap, transfer onto warm serving plates and enjoy!

Each week after football training our son Jack seems to bring half the football team home with him. When they've been running around a pitch after a full school day, all the boys are usually starving, so they need feeding as soon as they're through the door. If it's a cold and wet day and the pitch was soggy, they usually crave hearty, warming, comfort food. At other times all they'll want is good, simple food that refuels them quickly.

I do believe that you have to play it safe when you have a full dining table – particularly when it's filled with other people's children – and I try to serve up food that I'm pretty confident they'll all eat, not just what I know my own kids will eat. When Jack's friends come over I tend to give them toad in the hole or sausages with vegetables. I might offer a gravy that I know my children like, but make it clear to their friends that they don't have to have it, or else I serve a good, classic onion gravy that will suit most tastes. Having friends at the table also means I'll probably adapt the usual bowl of fruit for dessert to include some ice cream or something.

Above all, I think that the most important thing about feeding my children's friends is to make sure that they don't feel uncomfortable at the dinner table or, worse still, go home hungry.

Cauliflower cheese and bacon quiche

A traditional family favourite presented in a quiche.

plain flour for dusting
375g pack of ready-rolled
  shortcrust pastry
1 cauliflower, cut into small
  florets
1 handful of frozen garden
  peas
100g/3$^{1}/_{2}$oz unsmoked
  bacon, cut into strips
$^{1}/_{2}$ white onion, peeled and
  finely sliced
3 large eggs
284ml carton of double cream
175g/6oz finely grated mixed
  Gruyère and Parmesan
  cheese
2 tbsp chopped fresh chives
freshly grated nutmeg
salt and black pepper

Serves: 4
Prep time: 20 minutes
Cooking time: 45 minutes

1   You will need a 23cm/9 inch fluted-edge tart tin, about 4cm/1$^{1}/_{2}$ inches deep with a removable base. Using a lightly floured rolling pin, roll out the pastry to about the thickness of a pound coin, slightly thinner if you can. Line the tart tin with the pastry, pushing it into the edges firmly, then trim off the overhanging pastry and put the base into the fridge to chill for at least 30 minutes.

2   Preheat the oven to 200°C/400°F/GM6.

3   Line the pastry case with baking parchment and fill with baking beans. Bake in the oven for 10–12 minutes until the pastry is slightly colouring, then remove beans and parchment and let it have another couple of minutes – don't let it colour too much. Remove the pastry case from the oven and turn the temperature down to 170°C/325°F/GM3.

4   Put the cauliflower into a steamer and steam for 5–7 minutes, then remove and put to one side.

5   Cook the bacon in a dry pan, allowing to colour just slightly but don't get too crisp. Add the onion and cook until softened.

6   In a mixing bowl, combine the eggs, cream, cheese, chives and nutmeg with a good grinding of pepper and a pinch of salt. Add the cauliflower, peas, bacon and onion and stir together until all is well coated. Take care to keep the cauliflower in florets.

7   Pour the mix into the pastry case and bake in the oven for 25–30 minutes – the pastry should be golden and the filling should shake a little; it continues to set once out of the oven so leave for 10 minutes before tucking in. Serve with a rocket salad drizzled with wholegrain mustard vinaigrette.

Herb-crusted pork fillet with creamed leeks

This is easy and delicious. What makes it particularly successful is the way in which the cream from the leeks mixes with the chopped herbs. I use whipping cream rather than double cream because it is lower in fat. Even so, this probably won't win any healthy-eating prizes, but then you don't have to eat it every day of the week!

15g pack of fresh rosemary
    or 8 large sprigs
2 tsp dried sage
4 tsp fennel seeds
400g/14oz pork neck fillet,
    sliced into discs about
    1.5cm/²/₃ inch wide
5 leeks, cleaned, trimmed
    and cut into slices 2cm/
    ³/₄ inch thick
30g/1¹/₄oz butter
150ml/5fl oz whipping cream
olive oil
salt and black pepper

Serves: 2-3
Prep time: 10 minutes
Cooking time: 10 minutes

1 Take a large chopping board and put the rosemary, sage, fennel seeds, a good pinch of salt and a grinding of pepper in the middle of the board. Chop everything finely with a sharp knife. Take each slice of pork and push into the herb mixture so that there is a covering of chopped herbs on each side.

2 Put the leeks into a frying pan, cover with water and season with salt. Bring to the boil, reduce the heat and simmer for 3 minutes. Drain the leeks. Melt the butter in the frying pan on a medium heat. Add the semi-cooked leeks and fry until they are just starting to colour at the edges. Add the cream and bring to the boil. Simmer for 3-4 minutes, until slightly reduced and thickened. Season with pepper and a little salt, if necessary.

3 While the leeks are frying, heat the oil in a second frying pan. When the oil is hot, add the pork discs and fry for 2 minutes on each side. Remove from the pan and serve immediately with the creamed leeks.

Roast pork loin with cannellini beans, pancetta and thyme

It is notoriously difficult to make decent pork gravy – the meat gives off very little juice while cooking, making it much harder to create tasty gravy the easy way. This recipe cleverly gets around the problem by creating a creamy sauce to accompany the roast pork from a combination of beans, bacon and fresh herbs. For more people simply get a larger joint!

1kg/2¼lb boneless pork loin joint

1 tbsp olive oil

200g/7oz piece of pancetta, diced

2 × 400g tins of cannellini beans, drained through a sieve and then rinsed

15g pack of fresh thyme, leaves removed and roughly chopped

½ chicken stock cube, dissolved in 300ml/½ pint boiling water

coarse sea salt, crushed, and black pepper

watercress to serve

Serves: 3-4
Prep time: 20 minutes
Cooking time: 1¼ hours (based on cooking the pork joint for 25 minutes per 450g/1lb and 25 minutes extra)

1 Preheat the oven to 220°C/425°F/GM7.

2 In order to achieve prefect crackling, make sure the skin of the pork is scored well, then dry it thoroughly with kitchen paper. Sprinkle with crushed salt.

3 Place the pork in the oven and set the kitchen timer for 30 minutes. When the timer beeps, turn the oven down to 180°C/350°F/GM4 and reset the timer for 45 minutes.

4 Meanwhile, make the sauce. Put a medium saucepan on the hob on a moderate heat. Add the oil and warm through. Add the pancetta, increase the heat and fry until the fat runs and the pancetta starts to crisp.

5 Add the cannellini beans and thyme to the pancetta and mix together. Season with pepper and remove from the heat.

6 When the pork has cooked, remove from the oven and leave to rest for 10-15 minutes. Meanwhile, immediately the pork is out of the oven, reheat the pancetta, beans and thyme. Add the chicken stock, return the saucepan to the heat and bring to the boil, stirring well. Season to taste. Remove 2 tablespoons of the beans, mash roughly and stir back in.

7 Slice the pork thickly. Spoon the bean mixture onto a plate and arrange the slices of pork on top. Garnish with watercress. Serve immediately.

We try to spend Saturdays and Sundays as simply as we can. Party invites are often turned down and getting together with extended family and friends is kept for special occasions. Usually none of us wants to go anywhere particular. It's being together that counts. Routine and rules are bent or broken and getting-up times can drift into mid-morning (unless we're all champing at the bit to get out somewhere, in which case Gordon or I will have to go and drag the late sleeper out of bed to keep everyone else happy!). So breakfast often becomes lunch, and lunch blends into an early supper.

Sometimes we'll head out of London and off to the beach, where the kids can pull on their wetsuits and hurl themselves onto their body boards while we sit on deck chairs reading the papers. Most weekends we're at home in London, though, where we'll spend the time catching up with each other and perhaps going for long bike rides through our local park. Gordon and I will often run alongside the kids on their bikes and try to keep pace with them. Then we'll stop in the park and have a drink and sit or clamber over fallen trees and logs before heading back home for a late lunch or nipping to the pub for an early supper.

Saturday nights usually end with a trip to the cinema or just lounging around at home. Because weekends are the times we give ourselves a treat, we'll make hot chocolate and popcorn or, the kids' current favourite, we'll pile up a tray with dips and crisps and sticks of vegetables and relax in front of a film.

Chorizo sausage tortilla with grilled pepper salad

Don't be concerned about the quantity of olive oil listed below. Most of it is drained off before eating, but the flavour it imparts during the cooking is vital to the success of the dish. It makes a wonderful alternative to sandwiches for a picnic.

250g/9oz chorizo sausage, peeled and sliced as thick as a one pound coin
250ml/9fl oz olive oil, plus a little extra for greasing
500g/1lb 2oz white onions, peeled and sliced
1 tsp smoked paprika
600g/1lb 5oz waxy potatoes, peeled and sliced as thick as a one pound coin
6 large eggs, beaten
30g pack of fresh flat-leaf parsley, leaves chopped
salt and black pepper

FOR THE PEPPER SALAD
6 peppers of all colours, quartered, deseeded and all white pith removed
1 tbsp white wine vinegar
3 tbsp olive oil
1 handful of roughly chopped rocket leaves

Serves: 5-6
Prep time: 20 minutes
Cooking time: 50 minutes

1 Make the pepper salad well in advance. Preheat the grill to hot. Arrange the peppers, skin-side up, on a baking sheet and put under the grill for 10-15 minutes, until the skin is charred and bubbling. Immediately they are out from under the grill, place the peppers in a freezer bag or plastic food container with an airtight lid. Seal and allow to cool until easy to handle. You will now find that the skins slip off easily. Cut the peppers into slices about 1cm/$^1/_2$ inch wide. Place in a bowl and season with salt and pepper. Add the vinegar and oil. When ready to eat, stir in the chopped rocket.

2 Put an ovenproof, non-stick frying pan on a medium heat and allow to warm through. Add the chorizo and fry until the fat begins to run and the sausage starts to colour. Remove the chorizo from the pan and put to one side.

3 Heat 50ml/2fl oz of the oil in the frying pan. Reduce the heat and add the onions to the pan. Cook for about 10 minutes until they are soft and translucent. Add the paprika and cook for a further 2 minutes, then add the remaining oil. Heat gently, then add the potatoes, stirring to coat them in the hot oil. Spread them out in an even layer, season well with salt and pepper and cook gently, turning occasionally, for 30 minutes until completely soft.

4 It is now necessary to remove any excess oil. Tip the contents of the pan into a sieve placed over a heatproof bowl and leave to drain for a few minutes.

5 Beat the eggs in a large bowl and season with salt and pepper. Add the onions, potatoes, chorizo and parsley to the eggs. Stir, trying not to break up the potato.

6 Warm the frying pan on the hob and add the merest dash of oil. Using absorbent kitchen paper, rub the oil around the bottom of the pan. Pour in the egg and potato mixture and cook over a low to medium heat for 15 minutes, until the tortilla is almost set but still slightly liquid on top. Meanwhile, preheat the grill.

7 Place the tortilla in the pan under the grill and cook for about 5 minutes, making sure the top doesn't burn. Remove from the grill and leave for 10 minutes. Loosen the edges with a palette knife and turn out onto a plate. Serve with the pepper salad.

Pork escalopes with spicy prune chutney

The chutney in this recipe keeps very well in the fridge for a couple of weeks and can therefore be made well in advance.

2 pork leg escalopes, each
   weighing about 250g/9oz,
   beaten to about 8mm thick
1 egg, beaten
8 tbsp wholemeal breadcrumbs
3 tbsp olive oil

FOR THE MARINADE
2 tbsp soy sauce
juice of 2 lemons
1 tsp honey
2 tbsp olive oil

FOR THE CHUTNEY
1 tbsp olive oil
1 medium red onion
1 Bramley apple
150g/5oz dried prunes, pitted
1½ tbsp soft brown sugar
50ml/2fl oz balsamic vinegar
300ml/10fl oz water
1 cinnamon stick, 2 star anise,
   and 1 whole dried chilli
salt and black pepper

Serves: 2
Prep time: 15 minutes plus
up to 2 hours marinating
Cooking time: 50 minutes

1. Begin by marinating the pork. Combine the marinade ingredients in a medium-sized bowl, add pepper to taste and add the pork. Turn to coat the pork with the mixture and leave for up to 2 hours.

2. To make the chutney, peel and finely dice the onion. Peel, core and finely slice the apple. Cut the prunes into quarters. Heat the oil in a medium saucepan and fry the onion on a low to medium heat until soft but not coloured. Add the apple and cook for 2 minutes. Add the prunes, sugar, balsamic vinegar and water, stir well and bring to the boil. Add the cinnamon, star anise and dried chilli and submerge. Reduce to a gentle simmer and cook uncovered for about 45 minutes, stirring often, until reduced and thick. Season with a little salt and pepper.

3. Ten minutes before you are ready to eat, remove the pork from the marinade and dry on absorbent kitchen paper. Dunk into the beaten egg, shake off any excess and then dip in the breadcrumbs to coat thickly.

4. Heat the oil in a frying pan until it is hot. Test the heat by adding a spare breadcrumb to the oil – if it spits and colours, the oil is ready for the pork. Add the meat carefully and cook for 3 minutes on each side, making sure the breadcrumbs are golden and crisp rather than pale and soggy. Drain on absorbent kitchen paper.

5. Remove the chilli, star anise and cinnamon stick from the chutney before serving and gently warm it through, if necessary. Make sure the consistency is not too solid – you may need to add a little water to loosen. Serve with the pork.

Sausages with apples and juniper berries

This is a real Saturday night supper on a cold winter's night. The secret is to make sure the sausages are the best possible quality, but even so, it's a very economical way of eating well. Serve with mashed potato with leeks and capers (see page 182) and Savoy cabbage.

2 tbsp olive oil

450g/1lb top-quality pork sausages

3 Cox's apples, peeled, cored and quartered

400g/14oz shallots, peeled (see 'Why Not Try...' on page 37)

275ml bottle of dry cider

1 tbsp juniper berries

15g pack of fresh thyme, leaves removed and roughly chopped

2 bay leaves

15g/^{1}/$_2$oz butter, softened

1 dspn plain flour

15g pack of fresh flat-leaf parsley, roughly chopped

salt and black pepper

1 Choose a large sauté pan with a tight-fitting lid. Warm the pan, then add the oil. Brown the sausages on all sides, then transfer to a plate and put to one side.

2 Add the apples to the hot fat and fry on all sides to a rich golden colour. Remove to the plate with the sausages.

3 Brown the shallots in the pan until they too have a good, even colour. Return the sausages and apples to the pan and add the cider, juniper berries, thyme and bay leaves. Bring to the boil, then reduce the heat, put on the lid and simmer for 15 minutes.

4 Work the butter and flour into a paste. Stir the paste into the pan, a little at a time. Stir well until the sauce has thickened and the sauce is once again bubbling. Simmer for about 5 minutes. Stir in the chopped parsley. Check the seasoning and add a little more salt, if necessary, and a good grinding of pepper. Serve immediately.

Serves: 3-4
Prep time: 25 minutes
Cooking time: about 30 minutes

Simply
VEGETABLES

I like to give the children their '5-a-day' of fruit and vegetables every day. In our house vegetables tend to be served as a side dish to something else – meat, fish or poultry – and don't often feature as the main element of a meal, but they will always appear in some form or another.

When I'm cooking at home on a busy night, I'll often toss a few extra vegetables into a dish at the last minute, or swap them with something else if I haven't got what I need in the fridge, or haven't made it to the shops or had my weekly shopping delivery yet. Wherever possible, I do like to cook using fresh produce that's in season, but when it comes to certain vegetables I think frozen can be just as good. In fact, recent research has shown that some fresh 'seasonal' vegetables that are for sale in supermarkets all year round have significantly fewer nutrients than frozen ones. This is basically because often the freezing process takes place within hours of the vegetables being picked, which means they retain their nutrients better than those that travel halfway across the world in refrigerated containers.

So don't hesitate to keep bags of frozen peas, sweetcorn, broad beans, or whatever, in your freezer – they can actually be the healthier option, not to mention easier, giving you the benefit of knowing you've always got them to hand, fresh, when you need them and not lurking half-dead in the bottom of the fridge.

Fresh peas, flageolet beans, red onion
   and mint salad

Asparagus spears with pecorino

Pruple sprouting broccoli with chillli
   and garlic oil

Spring greens with nutmeg butter

Spaghetti of carrots with cardamon butter

Beetroot and clementine salad

Cucumber pappardelle with dill

Courgettes with tomato sauce
   and chopped coriander

Buttered sweetcorn niblets with fresh
   marjoram leaves

Green beans with sun-dried tomato paste

Fresh peas, flageolet beans, red onion and mint salad

Wherever possible I use tinned beans, but in this case it really is better to use dried flageolet beans. You have to think a little in advance, but the process of rehydrating the beans is very straightforward. You'll need to start this the night before.

50g/2oz dried flageolet beans
4 tbsp extra virgin olive oil
1 medium red onion, peeled
   and finely diced
200g/7oz fresh shelled peas
15g pack of fresh mint, leaves
   roughly chopped
salt and black pepper

Serves: 4 as a side dish
Prep time: 5 minutes plus
overnight soaking
Cooking time: 1 hour
20 minutes

1 Soak the beans overnight in a bowl of fresh water. The following morning, rinse the beans in a sieve, then pour them into a saucepan, cover with water and bring to the boil. Reduce the heat and simmer without a lid for 1¼ hours. Drain the beans and rinse with cold water.

2 Warm 2 tablespoons of the oil in a medium saucepan. Add the onion and fry for about 1 minute to slightly soften but not to cook it.

3 Add the peas and stir well until the peas are warm. Stir in the flageolet beans and do the same. Add the remaining oil and season well with salt and pepper.

4 Remove from the heat, stir in the mint and serve immediately.

WHY NOT TRY…
Delicious with the rosemary-infused monkfish on page 88.

Asparagus spears with pecorino

You can use Gruyère or Parmesan with this, but I favour pecorino.

200g/7oz asparagus
olive oil, to drizzle
a handful of pecorino cheese
   shavings
salt and black pepper

Serves: 2
Prep time: 5 minutes
Cooking time: 10 minutes

1 Preheat the grill. Trim the base of the asparagus and peel the lower half of each spear.

2 Steam the asparagus for 5–7 minutes, depending on how thick they are, until just tender.

3 Transfer to a flat dish, drizzle lightly with a little oil, sprinkle a little salt and pepper on and toss over the shaved pecorino.

4 Place under the grill for 1–2 minutes, until the cheese has just melted, then serve.

WHY NOT TRY...

I love serving this with salmon. One of my favourite combinations!

Purple sprouting broccoli with chilli and garlic oil

If purple sprouting broccoli is not in season, use tenderstem broccoli instead.

400g/14oz purple sprouting
  broccoli
4 tbsp garlic-flavoured
  olive oil
2 large red chillies, deseeded
  and finely sliced
salt and black pepper

1 Cut the heads off the broccoli and put to one side. Cut two slices from each stem, each about 3cm/1¼ inches long. Discard the tough ends.

2 Heat the oil in a wok or frying pan and add the chopped stems. Stir-fry for 3 minutes. Add the chilli and broccoli heads and stir-fry for a further 2 minutes. Adjust the seasoning and serve immediately.

Serves: 4 as a side dish
Prep time: 5 minutes
Cooking time: 5 minutes

WHY NOT TRY...

Serve with the roast pork loin on page 139.

Spring greens with nutmeg butter

A simple twist on a classic English vegetable.

500g/1lb 2oz spring greens
   or spring cabbage
15g/$^1/_2$ oz butter
1 tbsp olive oil
freshly grated nutmeg
salt and black pepper

Serves: 4 as a side dish
Prep time: 5 minutes
Cooking time: 8–10 minutes

1 Trim the spring greens and cut them into 3mm/ $^1/_8$ inch strips. If using cabbage, quarter lengthways and cut out the stalk, then cut each quarter into 3mm/$^1/_8$ inch strips and wash well. Place the chopped cabbage into a steamer above a pan of boiling water and steam for 4–6 minutes until tender but still slightly crunchy.

2 Melt the butter in a medium saucepan. Add the oil and a generous grating of fresh nutmeg. When the butter and oil start to bubble, add the steamed cabbage and stir well.

3 When the cabbage is coated with the buttery nutmeg, season with salt and pepper, turn out into a bowl and serve immediately.

In our house the kitchen is the place where the kids really want to hang out. You might think that it is because Gordon and I love good food that our children also have that passion and are fascinated by food, but whether it's that or by their own choice, they are always magnetically drawn to the kitchen.

Whether I'm working and trying out recipes, or simply cooking our lunch or dinner, the children will hover and peer, fixated on what I'm doing, badgering me to let them help or asking for a taste of what's being prepared. They love food and trying out new things, and I think that's because we've always encouraged them to get involved. There are times, though, when I just want to get dinner cooked as quickly as possible so that I can get on with other stuff and so on these occasions it's easier to do it myself without their input; but when I have more time and I'm in less of a rush, I do always try to encourage the kids to get involved.

We want the children to learn to cook and have a good basic knowledge of food, so when the day comes that they leave home, they'll be able to fend for themselves and live a pretty healthy life. With children of different ages in our house, and still all relatively young, there's a limit to what they can do to help in the kitchen that isn't dangerous. Helping with food preparation is usually the safest bet, and quite often that means they end up stirring mixes or peeling carrots and potatoes for me while I cook. It's fun for them, and it's a help to me.

Spaghetti of carrots with cardamom butter

A great combination of two flavours – perfect with fish.

4 large carrots, peeled and
   sliced very thinly into strips
   like spaghetti
50g/2oz butter
4 cardamom pods, lightly
   crushed
salt to sprinkle

Serves: 4 as a side dish
Prep time: 10 minutes
Cooking time: 10 minutes

WHY NOT TRY...
**Serve with the sardines
on page 84. Perfect for a
summer's day!**

1   Steam the carrots for 5–7 minutes only, as they are
    very thinly sliced.

2   Meanwhile, melt the butter in a pan and add the
    cardamom pods.

3   Add the carrots to the pan and turn them to coat in
    the cardamom butter. Simmer gently for a couple of
    minutes. Remove the cardamom pods and sprinkle the
    carrots with salt flakes before serving.

Beetroot and clementine salad

Tasty and refreshing, an unbeatable combination!

400g/14oz cooked and peeled
   beetroot, cut into 5mm/
   $1/4$ inch slices
6 clementines, peeled and cut
   horizontally into 5mm/
   $1/4$ inch slices
4 tbsp olive oil
$1^1/_2$ tbsp white wine vinegar
15g pack of fresh flat-leaf
   parsley, leaves roughly
   chopped
salt and black pepper

1 Arrange the beetroot and clementines on a serving plate, alternating one slice of clementine with one slice of beetroot.

2 Put the oil, vinegar and parsley in a jam jar, put the lid on and shake together. Season with salt and pepper.

3 Pour the dressing over the salad and leave for at least 30 minutes before serving.

Serves: 4 as a side dish
Prep time: 15 minutes plus
30 minutes standing

WHY NOT TRY...

For a different twist, use mint instead of parsley.

Cucumber pappardelle with dill

Although this sounds fancy, it's actually very quick and easy to prepare.

2 large cucumbers
50g/2oz butter
2 tbsp chopped fresh dill
salt and black pepper

Serves: 4 as a side dish
Prep time: 10 minutes
Cooking time: 10 minutes

1 Wash the cucumbers and take hold of your lazy peeler (this is wider that a normal one, with a head about 2.5cm/1 inch wide. It's sometimes called a speed peeler). Slide the peeler the length of the cucumber – discard the first few slices until you get a good width on the slice. Continue slicing the whole cucumber, but discard the last few slices when they get scrappy again.

2 Heat the butter in a pan, toss in the cucumber slices and allow to gently warm through, then sprinkle in the dill and stir to gently mix. Season to taste and serve warm.

WHY NOT TRY...

Goes really well with fish, and is also great as a side dish with a selection of cold meats.

Courgettes with tomato sauce and chopped coriander

Courgette and coriander is an extremely tasty combination...

2 tbsp olive oil
3 courgettes, cut into slices
 about 5mm/¼ inch thick
3 tbsp passata
4 tbsp chopped fresh
 coriander
salt and black pepper

1 Heat the oil in a large frying pan, toss in the courgettes and cook over a medium heat for 5–8 minutes, until coloured on both sides and just tender. Add the passata, a sprinkling of salt and a grinding of pepper and allow to heat through.

2 Stir in the coriander and serve hot.

Serves: 4 as a side dish
Prep time: 10 minutes
Cooking time: 15 minutes

Buttered sweetcorn niblets with fresh marjoram leaves

Simple, simple, simple.

330g tin of sweetcorn niblets
50g/2oz butter
1 tbsp fresh marjoram leaves
salt and black pepper

Serves: 4 as a side dish
Prep time: 5 minutes
Cooking time: 5 minutes

1 Drain the sweetcorn and leave in the sieve while you melt the butter in a pan and pick the marjoram leaves.

2 Simply heat the sweetcorn in the butter with the marjoram leaves and serve warm – an amazing combination. Season to taste.

WHY NOT TRY...

This goes particularly well with a crispy chicken breast and sweet potato mash.

Although I was brought up in a home where my mother cooked everything from scratch, I was never really that interested in cooking when I was a child; it was more fun to be running around the fields and playing with my brothers and sister. Helping out in the veg garden or around the farm was only something that we did when it suited us, but we wouldn't offer too often. For a while everything was home grown or home made (I can remember a large glass jar in our kitchen with wooden paddles, in which my mum used to make our butter), but after a while even my mother realized it was just too much work and cut back on her self-sufficiency!

I like to make my life easier in simpler ways. Planning meals a week ahead is something that I find is well worth doing because it takes away the stress of wondering what to cook each night with hungry children asking when dinner will be ready. I look ahead at the diary and take into account what everyone is doing, what their nutritional needs might be and when they'll be home, and I try to anticipate what we'll feel like eating. My 'menu' won't be set in stone, and I'll always allow some room for flexibility should something unexpected crop up.

Unlike my mother, I won't make absolutely everything from scratch, as I think there are some 'cheat's' ingredients that are perfectly acceptable. I am very happy to buy ready-made pastry (I can't make pastry at all), frozen fruit and veg, and marinated peppers, for instance. To save me more time, I'll often order my shopping online and get it delivered.

Green beans with sun-dried tomato paste

I'm always trying to find new ways of serving up veg to my lot and this combination is one that always goes down well.

300g/11oz green beans, trimmed
1 heaped tbsp sun-dried tomato paste
salt and black pepper

Serves: 4 as a side dish
Prep time: 2 minutes
Cooking time: 5-7 minutes

1 Steam the beans over a saucepan of boiling water for 5-7 minutes until cooked but still crunchy.

2 Remove from the heat and put into a mixing bowl. Stir in the sun-dried tomato paste and stir well so that the beans are evenly coated. Season with a little salt if necessary and a good grinding of pepper. Serve immediately.

Simply
POTATOES

My favourite vegetable has got to be the humble potato – it's just such a fantastically good all-rounder – and it's one of the things my kitchen is never without.

Probably the reason I use potatoes so often is because they can be used in so many different ways and to accompany so many different dishes, or they can even be a meal in themselves – from comforting, fluffy mash and stuffed and hearty jackets, to sophisticated and indulgent dauphinoise. Armed with a bag of potatoes, I can always get something on the table for dinner, no matter how bare the cupboards.

Although my children will eat pretty much anything, that's not to say that they like absolutely everything they eat. Jack is the only one of them who is a bit funny about potatoes. He's happiest eating crushed new potatoes, which aren't difficult to do – I just boil some new potatoes until they are cooked, drain them and lightly crush them using the back of a fork. They are then tossed in a roasting pan with some olive oil or a couple of knobs of butter and cooked in the oven until they are browned and slightly crispy – a real comfort dish, and perfect any time of year with meat, chicken or fish.

Potato gnocchi

Bacon rösti cake

Bubble and squeak

Mashed potato with leeks and capers

Baked potatoes with succotash

Traditional dauphinoise potatoes

Sweet potato with mushrooms on toast

Crushed new potatoes with feta and mint

Roast potatoes with Taleggio and red onion

Cheese, spinach and potato pie

Potato gnocchi

Potato gnocchi, an Italian family classic, are surprisingly easy to prepare as long as you follow a few basic rules. It is important always to steam the potatoes rather than boil them, to prevent the potatoes from becoming waterlogged and, consequently, the gnocchi from becoming soggy. I use a hand-held electric mixer to mash the potatoes and mix in the other ingredients. You can use a normal potato masher, if you wish, but I think you get better results with the electric mixer.

1kg/2^1/$_4$lb floury potatoes, such as Maris Piper or Desiree, peeled and cut into even-sized pieces
200g/7oz plain flour plus extra for dusting
2 eggs, lightly beaten
50g/2oz Parmesan cheese, finely grated
salt

FOR THE TOMATO SAUCE
2 tbsp olive oil
300g/11oz baby cherry tomatoes
1 garlic clove, peeled and sliced
2 tsp aged balsamic vinegar (thick syrupy balsamic vinegar is best)
1 small handful of fresh basil, roughly torn
salt and black pepper

Serves: 4
Prep time: 15 minutes
Cooking time: 35 minutes plus 30 minutes chilling

1 Steam the potatoes for 20–25 minutes until tender. Meanwhile, lightly flour a baking sheet.

2 Remove the potatoes from the steamer and place in a large mixing bowl. Tip in the flour, eggs and Parmesan and mash together well using a hand-held mixer. Season well with salt.

3 Using well-floured hands, divide the mixture into four equal portions. One at a time, using your floured hands, roll out each portion on a floured surface into a sausage shape measuring about 2.5cm/1 inch in diameter. Cut each sausage into slices about 1.5cm/ ^{5}/$_8$ inch thick. Keep flouring your hands and the knife as you work. Push down each side of the gnocchi on the back of a grater and place on the baking sheet. Pop in the fridge for 30 minutes or more before cooking.

4 Meanwhile, make the tomato sauce. Heat the oil in a pan. Add the garlic and sauté for about 30 seconds, just long enough to flavour the oil, taking care not to burn the garlic. Remove the garlic from the pan and discard. Add the tomatoes and cook over a gentle heat until they begin to soften and split. Stir in the balsamic vinegar and season with salt and pepper. Just before serving, stir through the torn basil.

5 Cook the gnocchi in small batches, adding them to already boiling, well-salted water. As the gnocchi rise to the surface, remove them with a slotted spoon and place on a warmed plate to drain. Divide between four bowls and serve with the tomato sauce.

Bacon rösti cake

This is a delicious brunch dish served with poached eggs and toast.

700g/1¹/₂lb floury potatoes,
  such as Desiree or Maris
  Piper (about 5 medium-
  sized potatoes)
200g/7oz rashers of good-
  quality smoked streaky
  bacon
2 tbsp olive oil
1 medium onion, peeled and
  finely diced
15g/¹/₂oz butter
4 eggs
black pepper and a little salt

Serves: 4
Prep time: 40 minutes
Cooking time: 35 minutes

1 Peel the potatoes and, leaving them whole, place in a saucepan of cold salted water. Bring to the boil. Drain the potatoes and, when cool enough to handle, coarsely grate into a large mixing bowl.

2 Cut the bacon into matchstick-sized slices. Heat 1 tablespoon of the oil in a frying pan on a medium heat. Add the bacon and fry until it is just beginning to crisp. Add the onion, reduce the heat and cook until the onion is soft but not coloured.

3 Add the bacon and onion to the grated potato and mix together using a fork, or if you prefer, your hands. Season well with pepper and a little salt – the bacon will be salty.

4 Heat the butter and remaining oil in a large, heavy-based ovenproof frying pan until sizzling. Add the potato mixture and, using the back of a spoon, push down and shape into a flat, solid cake. Fry on a low heat for 15 minutes until golden. Take a large plate and put on top of the frying pan. Tip the frying pan upside down so that the rösti sits on the plate, uncooked side uppermost. Carefully slide the rösti back into the frying pan and cook for a further 10 minutes until browned on the other side. Meanwhile, preheat the oven to 160°C/325°F/GM3.

5 Place the pan in the oven for 10 minutes while you poach the eggs. Cut the rösti into quarters and serve with the eggs and some toast.

Bubble and squeak

This is a great way of using up leftover mashed potato or Christmas leftovers. Having said that, I often deliberately make more mashed potato than necessary so that I can put some aside (either in the fridge, or bagged and frozen) for making these little burger-shaped treats. My favourite way of eating these is with a fried egg on top, although they also go well with roast lamb or rosemary-crusted pork chops.

300g/11oz Brussels sprouts, trimmed and dirty outside leaves removed
500g/1lb 2oz leftover mashed potato
100g/3^{1}/$_{2}$oz vacuum-packed chestnuts, broken into pieces
freshly grated nutmeg
1 tbsp vegetable oil
25g/1oz butter
salt and black pepper

Serves: 4
Prep time: 10 minutes
Cooking time: 20 minutes

1 Cut each Brussels sprout into three or four slices, through the root, depending on how large they are. Plunge into a saucepan of boiling salted water and cook for no more than 2 minutes. Drain and cool under cold water, then put to one side to drain thoroughly.

2 Put the mashed potato, Brussels sprouts and chestnuts into a large mixing bowl and mix well. Season with salt, pepper and a good grating of nutmeg. Using your hands, divide the mixture into eight and shape into burger-sized patties.

3 Heat a large frying pan on a medium heat. Add the oil and butter to the pan and when the butter is foaming, add the patties. Fry in batches until browned on either side – this should take about 5 minutes on each side. Serve.

WHY NOT TRY...

If you hate the idea of Brussels sprouts, use a seasonal choice of Savoy cabbage or spring greens.

Mashed potato with leeks and capers

Having tried making mashed potatoes by many different methods, I think you probably do get better results by steaming the potatoes, but I'm not despotic about it. I also like to use a potato ricer rather than a potato masher, since you are guaranteed to get smooth, lump-free results with very minimal effort. This is my all-time favourite mash.

1kg/2¼lb floury potatoes, such as Maris Piper, Desiree, King Edward, peeled and cut into even-sized chunks
75g/3oz butter
3 leeks, finely sliced
1½–2 tbsp small salted capers, to taste
100g/3½oz half-fat crème fraîche
a little milk
salt and black pepper

Serves: 4
Prep time: 25 minutes
Cooking time: 25 minutes

1 Place the potatoes in the top of a steamer over boiling water. Sprinkle with salt and cook for about 25 minutes, until tender.

2 Meanwhile, heat 25g/1oz of the butter in a saucepan, add the leeks and a little salt, then cover and cook gently for about 5 minutes, until tender. Remove from the heat and keep warm.

3 Tip the capers into a sieve and rinse under cold water, brushing off excess salt. Drain well and gently squeeze out the water.

4 When the potatoes are done, put the steamer basket in the sink for a few minutes so they dry off a little. Melt the remaining butter in a large saucepan over a low heat. Push the potatoes through a potato ricer into the pan (or add them directly to the pan and mash with a potato masher). Beat in the crème fraîche, followed by enough milk to give a soft mash. Fold in the leeks and capers, season with pepper and a little salt if necessary, and serve at once.

Baked potatoes with succotash

Everyone has their own idea of what makes the perfect baked potato, from the type of potato used to the ideal filling. This is my way with what I consider the perfect filling. Succotash is a great Native American recipe that I indulged in when we were last in the States – it is certainly very hearty and the kids loved it so much that I was forced to ask for the recipe!

4 deep, round, floury potatoes, such as King Edward or Maris Piper, each weighing 350–400g/12–14oz
fine sea salt
a little butter, to serve

FOR THE SUCCOTASH
150g/5oz rashers of streaky bacon, cut into strips
1 red onion, peeled and finely chopped
400g tin of butter beans, drained through a sieve and then rinsed
100ml/3$^{1}/_{2}$fl oz chicken stock
225g/8oz sweetcorn (I use frozen as it's crunchier)
3 tbsp double cream
1 handful of chopped parsley
salt and black pepper

1 Preheat the oven to 200°C/400°F/GM6.

2 Rinse off any mud from the potatoes and scrub them well with a vegetable brush and pat dry. Prick here and there with a fork then brush with olive oil and lightly rub some of the salt into the skin. Place in the oven directly on the rack and bake for about 1 hour. Check the potatoes are done by squeezing them gently – the flesh should just give a little.

3 Meanwhile, make the succotash. Fry the bacon in a large dry frying pan on a medium heat until crisp and golden and the fat runs. Add the onion, reduce the heat and fry until soft. Add the butter beans and stock to the pan and simmer for about 3 minutes, until the stock is reduced by half. Stir in the corn and cream and simmer for 3–4 minutes, until the corn is tender. Stir in the parsley and season with salt and pepper.

4 Using a small sharp knife, score a large cross along the top of each potato and squeeze the potato gently to open it up. Push in a small knob of butter, then serve the potatoes topped with the succotash.

Serves: 4
Prep time: 20 minutes
Cooking time: 1 hour

Traditional dauphinoise potatoes

You can't not like dauphinoise potatoes, a naughty addition to any meal (but you can argue that it is traditional!).

50g/2oz butter
1kg/2^1/$_4$lb Maris Piper
   potatoes or similar
150ml/5fl oz full-fat milk
142ml carton of double cream
2 garlic cloves, peeled and
   crushed with your hand
2 sprigs of thyme
pinch of nutmeg
25g/1oz Parmesan cheese,
   grated
salt and black pepper

Serves: 4-6
Prep time: 20 minutes
Cooking time: 1-1^1/$_4$ hours

1 Preheat the oven to 180°C/350°F/GM4. Use half the butter to grease a roasting tin or large gratin dish.

2 Peel the potatoes and leave in cold water until you are ready. Pat them dry and slice into thin slices 2-3mm/ ^{1}/$_8$ inch thick.

3 Put the milk, cream, garlic and thyme into a saucepan and heat to boiling. Leave to cool, then strain out the thyme and garlic. Add the nutmeg.

4 Layer half the potatoes in the roasting tin or gratin dish, seasoning each layer as you go with salt and a good grinding of black pepper. Pour half the milk mixture over this layer, then add the remaining potatoes and then the rest of the milk. Scatter the Parmesan on the top, dot with the remaining butter and bake in the oven for 1-1^1/$_4$ hours until the potatoes are tender and the top golden brown. Serve immediately!

WHY NOT TRY...

Make the liquid part in advance.

This dish is also very good reheated.

Even though my mother wasn't actually out in the fields in her wellies every day, she was still very much a working mother – managing the farm and all that went on in it – but she always made sure she was there when we got home. It's my memories of her juggling everything that have inspired me and guided me in how I look after my family.

I'm lucky that I can, quite often, work from home, and now that the children are at school all day I can juggle even working outside of the home with their school hours. Of course, there are times that I can't be there when they get back, but I always make sure that if it's not me at home, it'll be some other member of my family, as I'm fortunate to have my mother and sister living close by and we're always dropping in and out of each other's houses. And it's nice for the children to spend time with their grandmother, aunt and cousins, too.

When I am at home, as the children come through the door I do make a point of giving them my full attention and time, and so the phones are switched off and email is ignored. If I have to work, I make sure that it isn't at home – I don't think it's fair on them to come home and find me there, but not able to be with them. It's as hard for me as it is for them if I can hear them moving around the house while I'm trying to concentrate on something else.

As a working parent I think you always feel guilty that you can't be with your children when you think you ought to be – that's modern life – but if you're making the most of the time that you are together, that's all you can ask for.

Sweet potato with mushrooms on toast

A very strange sounding dish but so delicious. I first had it when I was in a very odd little café in the French Alps where I was skiing – the café was odd but the atmosphere and food were sensational!

2 sweet potatoes, peeled and cut into 2.5cm/1 inch chunks
olive oil
1 sprig of rosemary
1 knob of butter
100g/3½oz button mushrooms, halved
2 tbsp crème fraîche
1 small handful of chives
2 slices of granary bread
salt and black pepper

Makes: 2 slices
Prep time: 10 minutes
Cooking time: 25 minutes

1 Preheat the oven to 180°C/350°F/GM4. Put the potatoes into a pan of salted water and bring to the boil. Boil for 10 minutes and drain.

2 Transfer the potatoes to an oven tray and drizzle with a splash of oil. Sprinkle the rosemary over, add salt and pepper to taste, dot over the butter and place in the oven to roast for about 15 minutes, until soft enough to mash.

3 Meanwhile, heat a little oil in a frying pan and, when hot, add the mushrooms and a little seasoning. Cook for 10 minutes or so until golden.

4 Take the potatoes out of the oven and place in a mixing bowl. Mash roughly with the back of a fork.

5 Mix the crème fraîche with the chives.

6 Toast the bread and spread the crème fraîche mixture onto it. Spread with the sweet potato mash and top with the mushrooms. Serve.

Crushed new potatoes with feta and mint

The mint really lifts these potatoes and gives a fresh twist to them.

900g/2lb new potatoes,
   scrubbed
olive oil
125g/4oz feta, broken into
   chunks
zest and juice of $^1/_2$ lemon
3 tbsp chopped fresh mint
salt and black pepper

Serves: 4
Prep time: 15 minutes
Cooking time: about
45 minutes

1 Preheat the oven to 190°C/375°F/GM5.

2 Put the potatoes into a large pan of water with a pinch of salt. Bring to the boil and cook until they are just slightly underdone – about 12 minutes.

3 Tip the potatoes into a large baking tray and crush them lightly with the back of a fork. Drizzle over a little oil, sprinkle over the feta, lemon zest and mint, squeeze over the lemon juice and gently mix all through.

4 Cook in the oven for about 25 minutes, until the potatoes are beginning to turn golden and crisp around the edges. Add a sprinkling of pepper and serve!

Roast potatoes with Taleggio and red onion

Oh, how to make roasties even more indulgent!

6 medium-sized floury
   potatoes (ideally Desiree),
   unpeeled
2 tbsp goose fat (you can, if
   you prefer, use half goose fat
   and half oil, but it is not
   quite as indulgent)
4 red onions, peeled and cut
   into wedges
200g/7oz Taleggio cheese,
   cut into small strips
salt and black pepper

Serves: 4
Prep time: 25 minutes
Cooking time: about 1 hour
(depending on size of your potato
chunks)

1 Preheat the oven to 240°C/475°F/GM9, or as hot as your oven will go.

2 Cut the potatoes into quarters or sixths, depending on the size, and place in a large pan of water with a generous helping of salt – this stage is where the salt really infuses the potatoes. Bring to the boil and boil for 5 minutes. Drain the potatoes in a colander, then return them to the pan and place back on the heat for a minute, shaking the potatoes to ensure all the water has gone.

3 Meanwhile, put the goose fat in a large roasting tin – you need about 3mm/⅛ inch of fat in the bottom of the tin. Place in the oven. When the tin is really hot and smoking, remove from the oven, carefully add the potatoes and sprinkle over with more salt – be generous. Turn the oven down to 190°C/375°F/GM5.

4 Return the tin to the oven and leave for 20–25 minutes, until the underside of each potato really crisps up. At this stage add the onion wedges and turn over the potatoes. Cook for about 15 minutes, then add the chunks of Taleggio. Cook for a further 15–20 minutes.

5 When the potatoes are golden and crisp, the Taleggio is bubbling and browning, and the onions are blistering, you know you are ready! Sprinkle with pepper and serve in a large serving dish. Indulge!

Cheese, spinach and potato pie

I first had this in Greece one summer – it was an instant hit with the children and ended up being requested most lunchtimes! In Greece they make it with feta, but I make it with Cheddar to give it an English twist.

25g/1oz butter plus extra for greasing
2 × 375g packs of ready-rolled puff pastry
1 egg, lightly beaten
plain flour for dusting
1 large onion, peeled and finely sliced
2 medium potatoes, peeled and finely sliced
250g/9oz spinach
225g/8oz mature Cheddar cheese, thinly sliced
salt and black pepper

Serves: 6-8
Prep time: 45 minutes
Cooking time: 40-45 minutes

1 Preheat the oven to 190°C/375°F/GM5. Lightly grease a rectangular baking sheet.

2 Unroll the sheets of pastry and lay them flat. Place one on the baking sheet as the base of your pie. Brush the outside edges with the eggwash. Using a lightly floured rolling pin, roll out the second sheet of pastry until it is about 1cm/^{1}/$_2$ inch bigger all round than the first sheet, then set aside.

3 Melt the butter in a large frying pan on a low heat and add the sliced onion and potatoes. Cover and cook gently for 8-10 minutes, until softened, stirring occasionally. Set aside to cool.

4 Meanwhile, in a hot non-stick frying pan, stir the spinach on a low heat until wilted. Drain and gently squeeze out any excess moisture.

5 Arrange the cooked onion and potatoes over the bottom sheet of pastry, leaving the eggwashed border bare. Season with salt and pepper. Arrange the spinach on top, then scatter the cheese over.

6 Loosely roll the remaining sheet of pastry onto the floured rolling pin and unravel it carefully on top of the pie. Gently press it down onto the eggwashed edges of your pie base so that the contents are sealed in. Trim the edges to neaten, then brush the top of the pastry with the eggwash. Place in the oven for 35-40 minutes. After this time the pie should be golden brown.

7 Cool for 15 minutes, then cut into large squares and serve with a delicious green salad!

Simply
PIZZA & PASTA

We try to keep as many weekends as possible simply as family time, so that we can all be together, just the six of us, and hide away from work or chores. Even if we do meet up with friends and family on a weekend, whatever we're doing will always be far more relaxed than our manic running about during the week.

And that goes for the food, too. Weekends allow me to prepare food slowly and without the time pressures of a working week. In our house, Saturday nights are often pizza nights, and this is a dinner the kids love to get involved with preparing. I can make up the bases and then each of them picks their favourite toppings from the cupboards or fridge, or sometimes tries something new, and piles them up ready for me to pop in the oven.

My other life-saving dish, any day of the week, any time of year, is pasta. It's quick and easy to prepare and can be as light or as heavy as you want or need it to be. Dress it up, dress it down, pasta can be as rustic or as posh as you like, depending on who you're trying to impress! It's a brilliantly hassle-free way of cooking, and you can adapt most recipes or sauces to include pretty much anything that's to hand – which is ideal when you're home late, back from a weekend away, or haven't made it to the shops. If you've got some dried pasta in the cupboard, you'll always be just minutes away from a delicious, nutritious meal.

Cavatappi pasta with Parma ham, petits pois and sun-dried tomatoes

Spaghetti with cod in a chilli, garlic and white wine sauce

Linguine puttanesca

Penne with fresh tomato, chilli and prawns

Rigatoni with purple sprouting broccoli and pancetta

Pappardelle with butter, mushrooms, parsley and garlic

High summer spaghetti

Linguine with crab and chilli

Seafood pasta

Ciabatta bruschetta

Mini pizzas

French bread pizza

Cavatappi pasta with Parma ham, petits pois and sun-dried tomatoes

A rather posh, creamy, cheesy pasta! You could use salami or normal ham if you prefer.

225g/8oz dried cavatappi, or similar spiral-shaped pasta
2 tbsp olive oil plus extra for drizzling
2 slices of stale bread
1 garlic clove, finely chopped
6 sun-dried tomatoes, cut into strips
250ml/9fl oz double cream
50g/2oz Parmesan cheese, freshly grated
4 slices of Parma ham, torn into strips
1 small handful of fresh basil leaves
black pepper

Serves: 4
Prep time: 15 minutes
Cooking time: 15 minutes

1 Cook the pasta in a large pan of salted boiling water as instructed on the packet.

2 Meanwhile, heat the oil in a frying pan then lightly fry the garlic. Whiz the bread in a food processor until you have fairly fine crumbs and add to the frying pan. Stir on a medium heat until the crumbs are crisp and golden, then remove from the heat and stir in the sun-dried tomatoes.

3 Gently heat the cream in a small pan, then add the Parmesan and stir until melted. Add a good grinding of black pepper.

4 Drain the pasta well, place back in the pan, drizzle over some olive oil and grind over some black pepper. Stir through the cream mix and add the Parma ham and basil. Stir all through, then sprinkle over the breadcrumbs and sun-dried tomatoes. Serve into warm pasta bowls.

Spaghetti with cod in a chilli, garlic and white wine sauce

A good supper for a lazy night.

300g/11oz haddock or cod
4 slices of stale bread
2 tbsp olive oil
500g/1lb 2oz dried spaghetti
3 garlic cloves, peeled and
 finely chopped
3 tsp dried chilli flakes
splash of white wine
zest and juice of $^1/_2$ lemon
3 tbsp chopped fresh parsley
salt and black pepper

Serves: 4
Prep time: 15 minutes
Cooking time: 20 minutes

1 Cut the fish into four even-sized pieces to make the cooking times the same.

2 Put the bread into a food processor and whiz until you have fairly coarse but even breadcrumbs. Heat 1 tablespoon of oil in a frying pan, tip in the bread-crumbs and allow them to toast until crisp and golden.

3 You need to be quite organized and have all your ingredients to hand now. Place the pasta on to cook in a large pan of salted boiling water as instructed on the packet. Season the fish.

4 Heat the remaining oil in a large frying pan and add the garlic, chilli flakes and wine. Add the fish and lemon zest. Allow the wine mixture to come to the boil, turn the pieces of fish over and reduce the heat so that the wine is just simmering. After about 1 minute, take out the fish using a slotted spoon and put to one side. The fish should be just cooked.

5 Let the wine mixture simmer for another 3 minutes or so until it has reduced by about one-third. Add a ladle of the pasta water to this.

6 Drain the pasta, once ready, and add it to the wine in the pan. Increase the heat until it is bubbling again, then add the fish and sprinkle in the parsley. Gently flake the fish throughout the pasta, add the lemon juice and toss thoroughly.

7 Serve in warm pasta bowls, adding a little more parsley on top and a scattering of the golden breadcrumbs as desired.

Sport is a really big part of our children's lives, and most of their out-of-school activities are usually spent training or playing football, tennis, or swimming. Most of these commitments are after school, but in Jack's case once a week he has an early morning start with swimming training.

I also like sport, and going for a run is one of the things I really like doing – if I get some spare time when I can do something for me without feeling guilty about all the other jobs I should be doing. Gordon also enjoys running whenever he has time, and we try to run together and with the kids. We've also both run the London Marathon, so we know how important it is to be fit and prepared for any sporting activity. One thing we found when doing our training is how beneficial it was to eat foods packed with carbohydrates, because this would keep our energy levels up and allow the energy we needed to stay the course to be released slowly.

So, the night before an early start, or before a long day with some important match at the end of it, I like to give the kids an energy boost with a carbohydrate-packed pasta dish. It helps them get up and get on with the day the next morning, and it makes me happy to know that I've done my best to prepare them for the tiring day ahead.

Linguine puttanesca

This is my take on a classic pasta dish – it always disappears in a flash!

4 tbsp olive oil plus extra for drizzling

2 large garlic cloves, peeled and finely chopped

1 large red onion, peeled and chopped

1 red chilli, deseeded and finely chopped

8 marinated anchovies, finely chopped

100g/3½oz pitted black olives, finely chopped

3 tbsp capers, rinsed and drained

250g/9oz cherry tomatoes, halved

400g/14oz dried linguine

1 handful of fresh basil leaves, torn

salt and black pepper

Serves: 4 hungry people
Prep time: 15 minutes
Cooking time: 20 minutes

1 Heat the oil in a large frying pan and fry the garlic, onion and chilli for about 5 minutes, until softened. Stir in the anchovies and cook gently for 1–2 minutes, until the anchovies dissolve. Add the olives, capers and tomatoes and cook, stirring occasionally, for about 5 minutes, until the tomatoes have softened.

2 Meanwhile, cook the pasta in a large pan of salted boiling water as instructed on the packet, until al dente. Drain the pasta well, return to the pan and drizzle with oil, then add a good grinding of black pepper.

3 Add the sauce to the pasta pan and stir all through. Sprinkle in the basil leaves and serve into warm pasta bowls.

Penne with fresh tomato, chilli and prawns

The tomato sauce here requires simmering for about 30 minutes, but other than that, it is very simple to cook and fast to pull together. The tomato sauce itself can be made in advance and also tastes wonderful on its own. It's a really useful standby.

500g/1lb 2oz plum tomatoes
$^1/_2$ tsp caster sugar
4 tbsp olive oil
1 small onion, peeled and very finely chopped
2 garlic cloves, peeled and finely sliced
225g/8oz dried penne
300g/11oz frozen raw tiger prawns, defrosted
1 mild red chilli, deseeded and very finely chopped
15g pack of fresh flat-leaf parsley, leaves chopped
15g pack of fresh basil, leaves torn
salt and black pepper
a little freshly grated Parmesan cheese, to serve

Serves: 2
Prep time: 20 minutes
Cooking time: 40 minutes

1 Lightly cut a small cross into the bottom of each tomato and put into a heatproof bowl. Cover with boiling water and leave for about 1 minute. Drain, cover the tomatoes with very cold water and leave for a minute or so. Remove from the water and slip off the skins. Cut each tomato in half and remove the stem, then dice.

2 In a large saucepan, heat about 3 tablespoons of the oil on a medium heat. Fry the onion until soft but not coloured – make sure it doesn't burn. Add the garlic and cook for 1 minute. Add the tomatoes and the sugar. Bring to the boil and reduce the heat a little. The sauce should be boiling fairly rapidly in order to quickly reduce. Cook for about 30 minutes until the sauce is thick. Check the seasoning and add salt and pepper as necessary.

3 When you are about 10 minutes away from wanting to eat, bring a pan of salted water to the boil. Add the penne and stir well. Reduce the heat a little and boil for 8 minutes. When the pasta has cooked for 5 minutes, put a large frying pan or wok onto a high heat. When the pan is hot, add the remaining oil. When the oil is shimmering, add the prawns and stir-fry for 3 minutes until they are pink and just cooked. Add the chilli and parsley and stir well. Add the thick, intensely flavoured tomato sauce and the basil and mix well.

4 The pasta should by now be cooked perfectly. Drain, leaving a little water clinging to each tube. Quickly add the pasta to the frying pan or wok and stir in. Serve with freshly grated Parmesan.

Rigatoni with purple sprouting broccoli and pancetta

This is a very quick after-work supper. It really is easier than picking the telephone up and ordering a take-away!

1 tbsp olive oil
125g/4oz pancetta, cubed
100ml/3¹/₂fl oz dry white wine
225g/8oz dried rigatoni
200g/7oz purple sprouting broccoli or tenderstem broccoli florets
2 tbsp half-fat crème fraîche
a little grated Parmesan cheese
salt and black pepper

Serves: 2
Prep time: 10 minutes
Cooking time: 20 minutes

1 Bring two large pans of salted water to the boil.

2 Heat a frying pan on a medium heat. Add the oil and, when it starts to shimmer, add the pancetta and fry gently until it starts to brown. Pour off any excess fat. Increase the heat, add the wine and stir well. Allow to boil until the wine has evaporated and there are only about 2 tablespoons of liquid left. Remove from the heat and put to one side.

3 When the water boils, add the rigatoni to one saucepan. Stir and leave to boil as instructed on the packet.

4 Add the broccoli to the other saucepan and bring back to the boil. Simmer for no more than 2 minutes. Drain the broccoli and return to the saucepan, then add the cooked pancetta and reduced wine. Stir in the crème fraîche and season with a good grinding of pepper (it shouldn't be necessary to use any salt due to the inherent salt of the pancetta).

5 As soon as the rigatoni has cooked, drain quickly, leaving a little water clinging to the pasta. Add to the saucepan containing the broccoli and pancetta and stir well.

6 Divide between two warm dishes, sprinkle with Parmesan and serve immediately.

Pappardelle with butter, mushrooms, parsley and garlic

This recipe probably won't appeal to the most health-conscious due to the amount of butter needed. However, without the butter the taste just isn't as good. So, in short, not perhaps a dish to have every day, but once in a while it won't do anyone any harm. The other advantage, of course, is that it is incredibly quick to cook. The secret is not to cook the pasta entirely before adding to the mushroom mixture – the pasta should finish cooking in the mushroom juices and therefore really absorb the intense flavours.

40g/1½oz butter
3 tbsp extra virgin olive oil
125g/4oz dark button
  mushrooms, sliced
50g/2oz oyster mushrooms,
  sliced
50g/2oz shiitake mushrooms,
  sliced
3 garlic cloves, peeled and
  crushed
225g/8oz dried pappardelle
20g pack of fresh flat-leaf
  parsley, stalks removed and
  leaves coarsely chopped
salt and black pepper
freshly grated Parmesan
  cheese, to serve

Serves: 2
Prep time: 10 minutes
Cooking time: 15–20 minutes

1 Put a large pan of salted water on to boil.

2 Choose another large saucepan with a tight-fitting lid and melt the butter with the oil. When it is very hot, add all the mushrooms. Stir well, making sure every bit of mushroom is coated with the butter and oil. Stir in the garlic, put the lid on the pan and remove from the heat.

3 Add the pappardelle to the boiling water. Check the cooking instructions on the packet for the pasta and however long it says the pasta will take to cook, take off 3 minutes from the time and set the kitchen timer accordingly.

4 When the timer beeps, take a ladleful of the pasta cooking water and add it to the mushrooms. Drain the pasta and add to the mushrooms, then return to a medium heat. Stir the pasta and mushrooms together and allow to simmer gently for 3 minutes until the pasta is cooked.

5 Stir through the parsley and a good grinding of pepper. Season with a little salt and serve immediately with the Parmesan.

High summer spaghetti

Imported tomatoes in winter won't have the flavour necessary to make this dish successfully. If you don't fancy using cherry tomatoes, substitute about 4 good-sized, intensely flavoured tomatoes, but make the effort to peel them first, before dicing them (see page 206, step 1).

225g/8oz dried spaghetti
3–4 tbsp extra virgin olive oil
1/2 small red onion, peeled and finely diced
250g/9oz vine-ripened cherry tomatoes, halved through the stalk
1/2 tsp caster sugar
1 small handful of fresh basil leaves, roughly torn
salt and black pepper

Serves: 2
Prep time: 5 minutes
Cooking time: 5 minutes

1 Cook the pasta in a large pan of salted boiling water as instructed on the packet.

2 Meanwhile, warm the oil in a medium saucepan. Add the onion and cook for no more than 1 minute. Increase the heat, add the tomatoes and sugar and gently stir together, being careful not to mush up the tomatoes. Season with salt and pepper. Add the basil and cook for about 30 seconds more. Remove from the heat.

3 When the spaghetti is cooked, drain and immediately add to the tomato mixture. Toss together lightly and drizzle over a little more oil if necessary.

4 Divide between two warm pasta dishes and serve immediately.

WHY NOT TRY...
Serve with shaved Parmesan scattered on top.

Linguine with crab and chilli

This is a beautiful, light, summer supper dish. It can be made equally successfully with tinned crab meat (just substitute two small tins of crab meat for the fresh crab in the recipe). It will taste slightly different, but will still be delicious.

225g/8oz dried linguine
250g/9oz fresh white
   crab meat
4 spring onions, finely sliced
1 small red chilli, deseeded
   and finely chopped
1 handful of rocket, finely
   chopped
20g pack of fresh flat-leaf
   parsley, leaves roughly
   chopped
zest and juice of 1 lemon
2 tbsp dry white wine
4 tbsp extra virgin olive oil
salt and black pepper

1 Cook the pasta in a large pan of salted boiling water as instructed on the packet.

2 Meanwhile, combine all the remaining ingredients in a mixing bowl. Season well with salt and pepper and put to one side.

3 As soon as the pasta is cooked, drain quickly and return it to the saucepan. There should be quite a bit of water still clinging to the pasta.

4 Return the linguine to a low heat, tip in the crab mixture and stir well. Check the seasoning and serve immediately in two warm pasta dishes.

Serves: 2
Prep time: 10 minutes
Cooking time: 10 minutes

Seafood pasta

A great dish to throw together when you don't have any fresh produce in the fridge. Of course, in Italy they don't normally serve Parmesan with seafood, but it's a combination my family really likes!

2 tbsp olive oil plus extra for drizzling
1 medium onion, peeled and finely chopped
2 garlic cloves, peeled and finely chopped
1 green chilli, deseeded and finely chopped
20 cherry tomatoes, quartered
1 handful of fresh basil and 4–5 leaves to garnish
150ml/5fl oz white wine
400g pack of frozen mixed seafood, defrosted and drained well through a sieve
400g/14oz dried spaghetti
salt and black pepper
generous amount of freshly grated Parmesan cheese, to serve

1 Heat the oil in a frying pan, add the onion, garlic and chilli and fry for 8–10 minutes, until the onion is soft but not coloured.

2 Add the tomatoes, tear in the basil, pour in the wine and bring to a vigorous simmer. Season with salt and pepper and simmer for about 5 minutes, then reduce the heat. Add the seafood mix and simmer very gently for about 5 minutes, until the seafood is thoroughly heated through.

3 Meanwhile, cook the pasta in a large pan of salted boiling water as instructed on the packet, until al dente.

4 Drain the pasta well, return it to the pan and drizzle with olive oil, then tip in your sauce and gently stir through.

5 Serve with a generous heap of Parmesan cheese and a few shredded basil leaves.

Serves: 4
Prep time: 20 minutes
Cooking time: 20 minutes

Ciabatta bruschetta

This makes a fantastic starter before a Saturday barbeque lunch or a casual weekend supper. Each topping listed is enough for one loaf of ciabatta. Freeze any leftover pesto.

1 × 300g loaf semi-cooked
   ciabatta bread
150ml/5fl oz garlic-flavoured
   olive oil
salt and black pepper

For the toppings

TOMATO AND ROCKET:
$1/2$ medium red onion
1 garlic clove
200g/7oz cherry tomatoes
2 tbsp extra virgin olive oil
1 tbsp balsamic vinegar
1 handful of rocket leaves

AUBERGINE CAVIAR:
1 medium aubergine
1 garlic clove
juice of $1/2$ lemon
2 tbsp olive oil
1 tbsp Greek yoghurt
mint sprigs, to garnish

PESTO:
2 garlic cloves
2 tbsp pine nuts
100g/$3^1/_2$oz fresh basil leaves
12 tbsp extra virgin olive oil
75g/3oz Parmesan cheese

Serves: 4 (in a selection)
Prep time: 10 minutes
Cooking time: 10 minutes

1 Preheat the oven to 180°C/350°F/GM4. Cut the crusts off the ciabatta and discard. Cut the loaf into slices about 1cm/$1/2$ inch thick and generously brush each side with the oil. Place on a baking tray and bake in the oven for 7 minutes. Turn each slice over and cook for 7 minutes. Transfer to a wire rack to cool.

2 To make the tomato and rocket topping, peel and finely dice the onion and put into a mixing bowl. Peel and crush the garlic, add to the bowl and mix well. Cut the tomatoes into quarters and carefully stir in with the oil and balsamic vinegar. Season with salt and pepper. Chop the rocket and stir in. Check the seasoning and spoon a generous dollop of tomato onto each piece of toasted ciabatta.

3 To make the aubergine caviar, preheat the oven to 190°C/375°F/GM5. Stab the aubergine several times, then cook in the oven for 15 minutes until the skin starts to darken and the aubergine wilts. Remove from the oven and allow to cool. Cut the stalk off the aubergine and peel off the skin. Using a sieve and your hands, squeeze out as much liquid as possible from the aubergine. Peel and crush the garlic. Place the aubergine pulp, garlic, lemon juice, oil and yoghurt in the bowl of a food processor and pulse until smooth. Season well with salt and pepper. Spoon the aubergine onto the bruschetta and garnish with a sprig of mint.

4 To make the pesto, peel and crush the garlic. Put into a food processor with the pine nuts, basil and oil and blitz until smooth. Grate the Parmesan, stir in and season with salt and pepper. Spoon onto the bruschetta and serve.

Of course, as much as I believe in cooking for my family and do enjoy it, there are times when I want a night off. Some days I don't have the time or the energy – or I've simply not got myself organized and I really can't conjure up anything from the empty fridge and cupboards.

When there really is nothing in the house, or we're home so late that I've lost the will to cook, we'll reach for a take-away menu and order up a curry, a Chinese, or perhaps a pizza. And there's nothing wrong with that – every once in a while. In fact, it's by taking the children to restaurants and on holidays abroad that they've been exposed to different flavours and foods, and because of this their tastes are now much more varied and demanding and they really want to try new things. The only downside is that when we get home from these exotic feasts they want me to cook the same thing again for them, which means I have to get back in the kitchen and start experimenting with combining meat, chicken or fish with a wide range of other ingredients and flavours in order to ring the changes and keep everyone happy.

I'll usually pare the dish down to a simpler form and put a more 'domestic' spin on something a bit 'cheffy'; often these recipes won't work first time, but by trial and error I can usually come up with something that will please most of the family! But if, after several attempts and a kitchen full of dirty dishes, I simply can't recreate an authentic Thai dish, for example, it'll be time to reach for that take-away menu again...

Mini pizzas

Children love these and they are a great way to introduce them to new flavours.

300g/11oz strong white flour
1 tsp (approx 5g) easy-blend
   dried yeast
1 tsp caster sugar
1 tsp salt
200ml/7fl oz lukewarm water
1 tbsp olive oil
plain flour to knead
400ml/14fl oz passata
300g/11oz mozzarella cheese,
   diced
extra virgin olive oil
salt and black pepper

TOPPING IDEAS
rocket and soft goat's cheese
capers, olives and anchovy
   fillets
ham and salami
mushrooms and ham
ricotta, Parmesan and
   Gorgonzola cheese

Makes: 6 small or 2 large pizzas
Prep time: up to $1^1/_2$ hours
depending on rising time
Cooking time: 12 minutes

1 Sift the strong white flour, yeast, sugar and salt into a large mixing bowl. Make a well in the centre of the flour and add the water and olive oil. Using a wooden spoon, start mixing the liquid and flour together. When a dough begins to form, use your hands to bring the mixture together. If the dough is too dry, add a little water. When the dough comes away easily from the bowl, turn out onto a floured worksurface. Knead with the heels of your hands, pulling the mixture out towards you and then bringing it back down into the middle of the dough again. Do this for 5 minutes until the dough is shiny and bubbles under the surface. Place the dough in a clean mixing bowl, cover with a clean tea towel and leave to rise in a warm place for about 30 minutes, or up to 1 hour at room temperature, until doubled in size.

2 Preheat the oven to 200°C/400°F/GM6. Line a baking tray with greaseproof paper.

3 When the dough is ready, sprinkle the worksurface with a little plain flour. Knock all the air out of the dough and knead for about 30 seconds. Divide the dough into 2 or 6 equal balls. Dust the rolling pin with flour and roll each ball out into a circle. Stretch it with your hands until it is as thin as you can make it, ideally about 5mm/$^1/_4$ inch thick. You are not aiming for a perfect circle – it will taste even better if it is authentically wonky.

4 Lay the pizza bases on the baking tray and spread a thin slick of passata on top of each. Add a topping of your choice. Sprinkle with mozzarella, season with salt and pepper and add a drizzle of extra virgin olive oil.

5 Place in the oven and cook for 12 minutes, until the crust is golden and the cheese is bubbling.

French bread pizza

This is an excellent way of using up slightly stale baguettes. My favourite way of eating them is to fold them in half fresh out of the grill to make a juicy calzone-style sandwich. Beware of burnt fingers!

oil for greasing

1 large baguette, cut in two
   then sliced in half
   lengthways

400g tin of chopped tomatoes,
   the juices drained off
   through a sieve

3 tbsp chopped fresh basil

a splash of Worcestershire
   sauce

black pepper

8 slices of honey roast ham,
   cut into strips

198g tin of sweetcorn, rinsed
   and drained

125g/4oz mature Cheddar
   cheese, grated

1 Preheat the grill and lightly grease a baking tray.

2 Place the baguettes cut-side up on the baking tray and lightly toast under the grill. Remove and set aside.

3 Put the tomatoes into a small saucepan with the basil, Worcestershire sauce and a good grinding of black pepper, and gently heat through over a low heat.

4 Spread the tomato mix evenly over the four baguette quarters, then layer over the ham and sweetcorn. Sprinkle the cheese on top and return to the grill until the cheese is bubbling. Serve immediately.

WHY NOT TRY...

Serve with a simple, fresh green salad on the side.

Serves: 4
Prep time: 15 minutes
Cooking time: 10 minutes

Simply
FRUIT

Come round to our house on a weeknight and you'll find every meal ends with a bowl of fruit. Of course, what's on offer will change with the seasons (although I am particularly partial to red fruit), and might be accompanied by some yoghurt or ice cream, but that's fundamentally it. The kids are quite happy, too, as they all love fruit – and that means they're getting their '5-a-day'!

Fresh fruit will always be on my shopping list, especially because we get through so much of it during the week, but I'm also not averse to having the odd tin of peaches in the cupboard to make a quick cobbler, or a bag of frozen fruit in the freezer to make a simple tart. They all have their uses, and they're not only just as healthy and vitamin-packed as the fresh option, but also brilliant if you suddenly find yourself wanting to make a dessert but have no fresh fruit or it's gone off already. Life's too short to get hung up on always having fresh fruit – and anyway, desserts are supposed to be a treat, not a hassle.

At weekends, though, when I have a little more time, my obsession with fruit will translate itself into a 'proper' dessert; how complicated this is will depend on who's eating it. Formal, posh desserts are reserved for when we're entertaining, whereas for everyday meals we'll usually eat more 'comfort-style' puddings.

Clementine tart

Peach cobbler

Oranges in red wine

Pineapple and mint sherbet

Lemon and meringue puddings

Tasty apple tarts

Banana tarte tatin

Maple syrup nectarines and warm
  raspberry sauce

Roast plums with cinnamon and lemon

Apple snow

Easy blueberry tart

Clementine tart

Simple, easy and always impressive!

plain flour for dusting
375g pack of dessert pastry
10 clementines
3 tbsp apricot jam
1 tsp water
5 star anise

FOR THE PASTRY CREAM
1 large egg and 1 egg yolk
25g/1oz caster sugar
20g/³/₄oz plain flour
200ml/7fl oz milk
³/₄ tsp pure vanilla extract
150ml/5fl oz double cream

Makes: 8 slices
Prep time: 30 minutes plus
20 minutes chilling
Cooking time: 20 minutes

1 Using a lightly floured rolling pin, roll out the pastry until it is about 3mm/¹/₈ inch thick. Use to line a 23cm/9 inch fluted flan tin with a removable base, pressing it well into the edges and trimming off the overlap with a sharp knife. Chill for about 20 minutes.

2 Meanwhile, preheat the oven to 190°C/375°F/GM5. Line the pastry case with baking parchment, fill with baking beans or rice and bake blind in the oven for 10-12 minutes, until the paper comes away easily from the base and the pastry is beginning to colour around the edges. Remove the paper and beans and return the pastry case to the oven for 4-5 minutes, until golden. Remove from the oven and leave to cool.

3 Next, make the pastry cream. Break the whole egg into a bowl and add the egg yolk and sugar, whisking with a hand whisk until the mixture becomes slightly thicker. After a minute of whisking, sift in the flour and whisk until all is incorporated. Gently heat the milk to boiling point, then whisk the milk into the egg mixture. Return the whole lot to the pan and whisk on a medium heat until very thick. Don't let it catch on the bottom of the pan - it will thicken very suddenly. Keep whisking until smooth, then cook for 2 minutes longer over a low heat, whisking gently to prevent it sticking. Remove from the heat and pour into a cold bowl, stir in the vanilla extract and cover the surface of the pastry cream with cling film to prevent it developing a skin on the top. Put to one side to cool.

4 Peel the clementines and remove any pith. Slice widthways through the centre into 1cm/¹/₂ inch thick slices. Put aside for the moment.

5 In another bowl, whip the double cream until it is getting stiff but not quite forming peaks. Fold this into the pastry cream as soon as it is cool.

6 Meanwhile, put the apricot jam into a small saucepan with the water and heat very gently until it loosens up enough to be able to 'paint' onto the clementine slices to glaze.

7 Line the cooled pastry case with the pastry cream. Arrange the clementine slices on top of the pastry cream, then brush the apricot jam lightly onto the clementines. Arrange the star anise on top and you are ready to serve!

Peach cobbler

This is a great storecupboard dessert. When you unexpectedly need to impress and look as if you are a perfect host, always turn to your tinned fruit – the ways you can present them are endless but always turn out delicious.

2 × 410g tins of peach halves
  in syrup
115g/3¾oz self-raising flour
½ tsp ground cinnamon
50g/2oz golden caster sugar
  plus 1 tbsp golden caster
  sugar to sprinkle on the top
60g/2½oz unsalted butter,
  chopped
1 egg yolk
60ml/2¼fl oz buttermilk
2 tbsp chopped hazelnuts
crème fraîche to serve

Serves: 4
Prep time: 20 minutes
Cooking time: 35–40 minutes

1 Preheat the oven to 180°C/350°F/GM4.

2 Put the peaches and syrup into a large saucepan and bring to the boil. Reduce the heat and leave to simmer to soften the peaches – about 10 minutes.

3 Put the peaches into an ovenproof dish, about 1.2 litres/2 pints capacity, along with half of the syrup.

4 Meanwhile, sift the flour and cinnamon into a mixing bowl and stir in the sugar. Rub in the butter with your fingertips until the mixture resembles breadcrumbs. Stir in the egg yolk and buttermilk until you have a slightly wet dough. Spoon the dough mix roughly onto the peaches in 6–8 dollops – the more rustic looking the better! Sprinkle on the hazelnuts and the remaining tablespoon of sugar. Bake in the oven for 25–30 minutes until nice and golden and the syrup is bubbling.

5 Serve with a large dollop of crème fraîche.

Oranges in red wine

Slightly more sophisticated ... maybe not for the kids!

1 bottle of fruity inexpensive
  red wine
175g/6oz caster sugar
2 star anise
1 cinnamon stick
2 sprigs of rosemary
5 large oranges
crème fraîche to serve

Serves: 4
Prep time: 10 minutes
Cooking time: 30 minutes

1 Pour the wine into a large saucepan and stir in the sugar. Pop in the star anise, cinnamon stick and 1 rosemary sprig. Bring to the boil, stirring to dissolve the sugar, and leave to boil rapidly for 20–30 minutes. The wine should have reduced by about two-thirds and be a fragrant syrup.

2 Meanwhile, slice off the top and bottom of each orange. Sit the orange on its flat bottom and carefully cut down the sides, removing vertical strips of peel. I find a serrated knife is easiest for this. Cut the oranges into slices about 7mm/$1/4$ inch wide. Arrange the sliced oranges in a shallow dish. Pour over the reduced red wine, removing the rosemary sprig, and leave to cool.

3 Decorate with the remaining rosemary sprig and serve with crème fraîche.

Pineapple and mint sherbet

A light and refreshing dessert offering – a perfect one to make a day or more in advance.
I particularly like eating this with a kiwi and strawberry fruit salad.

200g/7oz caster sugar
200ml/7fl oz water
1 medium super sweet fresh
   pineapple, peeled and cut
   into chunks
juice of $1/2$ lemon
3–4 fresh mint leaves, finely
   chopped, and a few fresh
   baby mint leaves to garnish

Makes: 500ml/18fl oz
Prep time: 20 minutes plus
freezing (at least 2 hours in a
freezer – overnight is best)

1 Start by making the syrup. Gently heat the sugar and
   water in a small pan until the sugar has dissolved. Set
   aside to cool.

2 Put the pineapple chunks into a food processor and
   blend until smooth. Transfer the pineapple pulp to a
   large bowl and stir in the sugar syrup, lemon juice and
   chopped mint until combined.

3 If you have an ice-cream maker, spoon the mixture
   into it and follow your machine's instructions. If you
   do not, pour the mixture into a freezerproof container
   with a fitted lid. Put it into the freezer for at least
   2 hours, removing to stir every 10–15 minutes until ice
   crystals have formed.

4 Remove from the freezer 15 minutes before serving to
   make it easy to scoop. Alternatively, remove it directly
   from the freezer and use a fork to scrape sherbet
   shavings over fresh fruit. However you choose to serve
   it, be generous! Garnish with baby mint leaves.

WHY NOT TRY...
**If you're in a hurry, cool the
sugar mixture more quickly
by pouring it into a bowl and
sitting it in another bowl
filled with ice.**

Lemon and meringue puddings

A classic pudding that will disappear in seconds! If you don't have crème brûlée dishes, use ramekins instead.

FOR THE LEMON CURD
30g/1¼oz cornflour
50g/2oz caster sugar
300ml/10fl oz water
zest and juice of 2 lemons
2 large egg yolks

FOR THE MERINGUE
4 large egg whites
200g/7oz caster sugar

Serves: 4
Prep time: 30 minutes
Cooking time: 35 minutes

1 Preheat the oven to 180°C/350°F/GM4. You will need four shallow individual crème brûlée dishes, each measuring about 11.5cm/4½ inches across.

2 To make the lemon curd, put the cornflour and sugar into a medium saucepan. Gradually stir in the water, mixing all the time, first into a smooth paste and then into a cloudy liquid. Add the lemon zest. Bring to the boil, stirring all the time. When it starts to boil, the liquid will become thick and lose its cloudy appearance. Simmer for a couple of minutes, then take off the heat. Add the lemon juice and stir well.

3 Put the egg yolks in a medium mixing bowl. Gradually pour the lemon mixture over them, stirring all the time. Mix well. Divide the lemon mixture between the crème brûlée dishes and put to one side.

4 To make the meringue, whisk the egg whites with half the sugar in a large clean mixing bowl until they form stiff peaks when you take the whisk out of the whites. Whisk in the remaining sugar, 1 tablespoon at a time, until it is all incorporated and the mixture is a beautiful glossy white.

5 Using a palette knife, spread the meringue over the lemon bases. Use the knife to make little peaks all over the top. Place in the oven for 30 minutes.

6 Allow to cool and serve either warm or at room temperature.

Tasty apple tarts

Apple pie is known in our house as Daddy's favourite dessert. When he was a child, it was what Helen, my mother-in-law, always cooked as a big treat, and whenever she comes to stay with us she cooks it for our children - Jack is a particularly big fan! Much to her disgust, I have come up with this recipe as a lighter option because sometimes the pastry on a traditional pie can be a little heavy - needless to say, Jack prefers Helen's version, but mine has gone down well as a dinner party dessert for those a little more concerned with waistlines!

oil for greasing
6 Cox's apples or similar
  variety with a slight bite
2 tbsp water
2 cardamon pods, lightly
  crushed
40g/1½oz soft breadcrumbs
125g/4oz sultanas
½ tsp ground nutmeg
½ tsp ground cinnamon
1½ tbsp golden caster sugar
zest of ½ orange
4 sheets of filo pastry
30g/1¼oz unsalted butter,
  melted
icing sugar to sprinkle

Makes: 8
Prep time: 15 minutes
Cooking time: 15 minutes

1 Preheat the oven to 200°C/400°F/GM6. Lightly grease a muffin tin.

2 Peel, core and slice the apples and put into a medium saucepan with the water and cardamom pods. Place on a medium heat, cover and cook, stirring occasionally, for about 5 minutes, until the apples have softened just slightly. Remove the cardamom pods, then add the breadcrumbs, sultanas, nutmeg, cinnamon, golden caster sugar and orange zest. Stir them gently through, then take the pan off the heat and put to one side.

3 Meanwhile, lay the filo pastry on a clean board. Brush one sheet with melted butter, then layer with another sheet, brush with butter again and continue in the same way with the remaining sheets, ending up with a buttered top. Cut the pastry into eight equal squares and lay at offset angles inside the muffin cases set in the tin.

4 Spoon the apples equally into the pastry cups and place in the oven for 10 minutes or until the pastry is nicely golden.

5 Transfer the tarts to a cooling rack and leave to cool. Dust with icing sugar to serve. Delicious warm with cream.

WHY NOT TRY...

Any leftover filling is delicious served with vanilla ice cream.

Banana tarte tatin

This pudding really is a revelation. Serve with good-quality vanilla ice cream for a very impressive and delicious treat.

175g/6oz caster sugar
50g/2oz unsalted butter
about 7 medium-sized
    bananas, peeled and halved
    lengthways
1 tsp fresh rosemary leaves,
    finely chopped
plain flour for dusting
375g pack of ready-rolled
    puff pastry

Serves: 6
Prep time: 10 minutes
Cooking time: 50 minutes
plus 5 minutes standing

1 Preheat the oven to 220°C/425°F/GM7.

2 To make the caramel in a saucepan, put the sugar and butter in a small, heavy-based ovenproof frying pan on a low heat and leave until the butter has melted. Stir until the sugar has completely dissolved, then raise the heat to medium and cook, tilting the pan occasionally, until the mixture becomes a rich, golden caramel. Pour immediately into a 20.5cm/8 inch diameter shallow ovenproof dish, being careful not to let the hot caramel splash. Arrange the bananas halves on top and sprinkle with the rosemary. Put to one side.

3 Using a lightly floured rolling pin, roll out the pastry and cut a circle about 4cm/1¹/₂ inches larger in diameter than the dish. Lay the pastry on top of the bananas and carefully tuck the edges down the side of the dish, gently pushing the bananas together as you do so. Place in the oven and cook for 40 minutes until the pastry is golden.

4 Remove from the oven and leave to stand for 5 minutes. Run a knife around the edge of the dish and invert a serving plate on top of the dish. Turn the dish and plate over and lift the dish off the caramelized bananas. Serve immediately with lashings of vanilla ice cream.

Maple syrup nectarines and warm raspberry sauce

The nectarines can be made up to 48 hours in advance and then refrigerated but make sure they come up to room temperature before serving. Serve with warm raspberry sauce and vanilla ice cream or fromage frais, depending on how healthy you are feeling.

6 nectarines, halved and
   stones removed
20g/³/₄oz unsalted butter,
   melted
100ml/3¹/₂fl oz maple syrup

**FOR THE WARM RASPBERRY
SAUCE**
70g/2³/₄oz caster sugar
75ml/2¹/₂fl oz water
juice of 1 large lemon
300g/11oz raspberries, frozen
   or fresh

Serves: 6
Prep time: 20 minutes
Cooking time: 20-30 minutes

1 Preheat the oven to 180°C/350°F/GM4.

2 Brush all sides of the fruit well with melted butter. Pack quite tightly into a shallow dish and drizzle with maple syrup. Roast in the oven for 20-30 minutes or until tender and golden brown. Put to one side until needed.

3 Meanwhile, make the raspberry sauce. Put the sugar, water and lemon juice into a saucepan and slowly bring to the boil, making sure all the sugar has dissolved. Simmer for 5 minutes.

4 Add the raspberries and stir well to defrost, if using frozen fruit, gently breaking up the fruit. Bring back to the boil and simmer for a further 5-10 minutes until the sauce is syrupy but not quite the consistency of jam. Allow to cool a little, then pass through a sieve, always being careful of hot sugar. Check that the sauce is sweet enough and add a little more sugar if necessary.

5 Arrange three pieces of fruit on each plate with a little of the syrup and artfully drizzle the raspberry sauce on top.

Roast plums with cinnamon and lemon

A great addition to a bowl of vanilla ice cream when you're curled up on the sofa ... or even served with goose or duck. The roast plums are quite tart, but if you are planning to serve them as part of a savoury dish, you might prefer to reduce the sugar by about 25g/1oz.

750g/1lb 11oz firm, dark
  plums
85g/3oz demerara sugar
$^1/_2$ tsp ground cinnamon
25g/1oz unsalted butter
grated zest of 1 lemon

Serves: 4
Prep time: 10 minutes
Cooking time: 25–30 minutes

1 Preheat the oven to 200°C/400°F/GM6. Halve and stone the plums, then arrange them in a single layer in an ovenproof dish, cut-side up.

2 Mix together the sugar and cinnamon and sprinkle over the plums. Dot with the butter, then scatter the lemon zest on top.

3 Place in the oven and bake for 25–30 minutes, basting with the juices a couple of times. When the plums are done, they should be very tender but still hold their shape.

4 Serve warm or at room temperature. The plums can be reheated in a low oven, if necessary.

For me, home-cooked is what I prefer to see on my kitchen table – but it doesn't always have to be my cooking ... Gordon will occasionally cook, but as he's been doing it all week, too, he wants to step back from that when he's home. Visiting family, however, are always more than welcome to get stuck in in the kitchen, and we all love the change of eating someone else's food.

As a mother, I'm always thinking about what I'm giving my family, and making sure that it's providing their five-a-day and everything else they need to grow, stay well, or simply get through a busy week. My cooking, particularly on school nights, is fundamentally practical and healthy, but when the grandmas cook, it's always wonderfully indulgent and a real labour of love.

The smell and flavours of my mother's cooking bring back memories for me of my childhood, and the same goes for Gordon. His mother loves cooking for us when she visits, and her onion gravy and mouth-watering apple pie are legendary. These meals are special family times that we all (especially the children) appreciate. Fortunately, the children also know that these are treats, so they don't spend weeks after grandma has gone badgering me to cook these dishes again!

Apple snow

Serve this light and fun pudding in individual tumblers or martini glasses, depending on how sophisticated you're feeling. Obviously this recipe contains raw egg, so it's not suitable for very young children or pregnant women.

6 eating apples, peeled,
   cored and sliced
50ml/2fl oz water
2 large egg whites
50g/2oz caster sugar
4 small sprigs of mint

Serves: 4-6
Prep time: 30 minutes

1 Put the apple slices and water in a medium saucepan with a tight-fitting lid and bring to the boil. Simmer over a very low heat with the lid on until the apples are very soft.

2 Drain the apples through a sieve and then blitz in a food processor to a smooth purée. Leave to cool completely.

3 Put the egg whites into a large bowl and whisk until the peaks hold their shape but the tops flop over. Whisk in the sugar, 1 tablespoon at a time. Carefully fold the apple purée into the egg white, a heaped tablespoon at a time. Divide between the tumblers or glasses, piling the snow high. Place in the fridge to cool.

4 Pop a tiny sprig of mint in the top of each glass before serving.

Easy blueberry tart

Ever since we were all told how amazing a superfood blueberries are, I have been rather obsessive about giving them almost daily to my children - usually simply mixed into yoghurt or in a fruit salad. When one of the children groaned at the thought of more plain blueberries being forced upon them, I thought it time to be a little more creative - but still quick and easy, of course...

plain flour for dusting
375g pack of dessert pastry
300g/11oz blueberries
1 tbsp golden caster sugar
200g/7oz mascarpone cheese
finely grated zest of 1 lemon
    plus juice of $^1/_2$ lemon
1-2 tbsp icing sugar, to taste,
    plus icing sugar for dusting

Serves: 6
Prep time: 15-20 minutes
Cooking time: 15 minutes
plus cooling

1 Preheat the oven to 200°C/400°F/GM6. Line a large baking tray with baking parchment.

2 Using a lightly floured rolling pin, roll out the pastry to about 5mm/$^1/_4$ inch thick. Use a dinner plate or the base of a cake tin to cut out a circle about 23cm/ 9 inches in diameter. Put onto the baking sheet and carefully prick all over with a fork, then pinch all around the edges with your thumb and forefinger. Chill the pastry base in the fridge for 10-15 minutes.

3 Meanwhile, put the blueberries into a saucepan along with the caster sugar and place on a low heat. You simply want to gloss the blueberries with the sugar and for them to soften ever so slightly, but not to get gloopy. Take off the heat and leave to cool completely, stirring gently occasionally.

4 Put the pastry base into the oven for about 15 minutes until golden, then remove and leave to cool completely.

5 Beat the mascarpone cheese with the lemon zest and juice and add icing sugar to taste. Once the base is completely cool, spread the cheese mix evenly over it, then spoon the blueberries on top. Dust with icing sugar and serve.

Simply
CHOCOLATE

Friday is treat day for the kids. Every day they take a snack to school, which is usually some fruit or a stick of cheese, but on Friday I like to give them a treat – especially if they've been good all week and done their homework and all their chores.

Usually I'll put a cookie or brownie in their snack box, and more often than not it'll be a little bit chocolatey. And then, if the children have friends coming over for tea after school, I might bend my fruit-for-after-dinner rule and instead give them a quick and easy pudding that's a little more of a treat and a bit less healthy. We all need a treat and I wouldn't want to disappoint!

After a good or bad day spent at school or work, you can't beat a good chocolate hit; the recipes in this chapter are not just for kids, we adults need a little indulgence, too. So go on and spoil yourself, dig into something really wicked...

Chocolate and beetroot cake

Chocolate and vanilla fancy biscuit bites

White chocolate cake with dark chocolate
topping

White chocolate-coated strawberry
ice-cream balls

Chocolate soufflé cake with cherries
and mascarpone

Chocolate bread and butter pudding

Chocolate pancakes

All-purpose chocolate sauce

Chocolate Malteser ice cream

Chocolate caramel slices

Chocolate and beetroot cake

This recipe belongs to Diana Henry. She made it on the TV programme *Market Kitchen* and I have to say I was a little sceptical of the beetroot element, but it is absolutely delicious and the beetroot gives it such an amazing texture, really keeping it moist.

125g/4oz unsalted butter, softened, plus extra for greasing
75g/3oz dark chocolate, broken into pieces
300g/11oz soft light brown sugar
3 large eggs, at room temperature
225g/8oz self-raising flour, sifted
$\frac{1}{4}$ tsp salt
50g/2oz cocoa powder, sifted
250g/9oz cooked beetroot, coarsely grated
grated white chocolate
crème fraîche, to serve

FOR THE ICING
150g/5oz dark chocolate, broken into pieces
142ml carton of soured cream
5 tbsp icing sugar, sifted
3 tbsp crème de Cassis (optional)

Serves: 10-12
Prep time: 25 minutes
Cooking time: 45-50 minutes

1 Preheat the oven to 180°C/350°F/GM4. Grease a 23cm/9 inch loose-bottomed cake tin and line the base with baking parchment.

2 To make the cake, put the chocolate into a heatproof bowl set over a pan of simmering water, making sure the water doesn't touch the base of the bowl. Leave until melted, stirring occasionally.

3 Put the butter, sugar and eggs into a mixer and beat until light and pale. Mix in the melted chocolate, then fold in the flour, salt and cocoa powder with a large metal spoon. Finally, stir in the beetroot.

4 Transfer the mix to the cake tin, make a slight dip in the centre with the back of the spoon and bake for 45-50 minutes. The cake is ready when a skewer inserted in the middle comes out with just a little of the mixture adhering to it. Leave the cake to cool in the tin for about 10 minutes, then turn it out onto a wire rack and leave to cool completely.

5 Put all the icing ingredients except the Cassis, if using, into a bowl and set it over a pan of simmering water. Leave to melt but don't let it overheat. Stir everything together, then take off the heat and add the Cassis. Stir really vigorously so that you are left with a smooth, glossy mixture. Leave to cool and thicken.

6 Spread the icing over the cake with a palette knife, then scatter with grated white chocolate. Leave the icing to set.

7 Serve with crème fraîche.

Chocolate and vanilla fancy biscuit bites

These really are the most amazing biscuits, they are so light they melt in your mouth and are terribly moreish...

350g/12oz unsalted butter, softened
75g/3oz icing sugar
1 tsp vanilla extract
300g/11oz plain flour
50g/2oz cornflour
25g/1oz cocoa powder, mixed to a paste with a little water

FOR THE SANDWICH FILLING
250g/9oz mascarpone cheese
1 tbsp golden caster sugar
20g/³/₄oz dark chocolate
2 drops of vanilla extract

Makes: 16 bites
Prep time: about 40 minutes depending on your piping skills!
Cooking time: about 15 minutes

1 Preheat the oven to 170°C/325°F/GM3. Line two baking trays with baking parchment.

2 Beat together the butter and icing sugar until pale and creamy. Add the vanilla extract and mix through. Sift in the flour and cornflour and beat until smooth. Halve the mixture, add the cocoa paste to one half and mix well. Add a little water to each mix if necessary. The mixture does need to be quite stiff, or the biscuits won't keep their shape. Spoon the mixtures into two piping bags fitted with star nozzles. Pipe 16 two-pound-coin size biscuits from the vanilla piping bag onto one baking tray, leaving a good space around each. Pipe 16 slightly larger rounds from the chocolate bag onto the other tray. Bake in the oven for about 15 minutes; do not overcook or they will be too dry. The vanilla biscuits should be lightly coloured on top and pale golden underneath; the chocolate ones should lift off the parchment easily and be dry to the touch. Once out of the oven, place immediately on wire racks.

3 Mix the mascarpone and caster sugar until smooth. Place two-thirds of the mixture in one bowl and the remainder in a separate bowl. Put the chocolate into a heatproof bowl over a pan of simmering water, making sure the water doesn't touch the base of the bowl, and leave until melted. Add to the larger mascarpone mix. Add the vanilla to the other mix and stir each mix through until smooth. Sandwich the biscuits together – the vanilla with the chocolate biscuits, and the chocolate with the vanilla biscuits, for contrast.

White chocolate cake with dark chocolate topping

Chocolate indulgence!

75g/3oz unsalted butter plus
   extra for greasing
300g/11oz digestive biscuits
300g/11oz white chocolate,
   broken into pieces
420ml carton of whipping
   cream, at room temperature

FOR THE SAUCE
100g/3½oz dark chocolate,
   broken into pieces
125ml/4fl oz double cream

Makes: 8 slices (more if just
making it for kids, as is very
rich!)
Prep time: 25-30 minutes
plus 1-2 hours chilling time

1 Grease an 18cm/7 inch loose-based round cake tin really well.

2 Put the biscuits into a food processor and whiz until they are smooth crumbs. Transfer to a large mixing bowl.

3 Melt the butter in a pan, then pour over the biscuit crumbs and stir to ensure all is covered. Press the biscuit mix well into the base of the tin with the back of a spoon. Put into the fridge for 30 minutes until firm.

4 Meanwhile, put the white chocolate into a heatproof bowl set over a pan of simmering water, making sure the water doesn't touch the base of the bowl. Leave until melted, then leave to cool.

5 Lightly whisk the whipping cream until it is forming very soft peaks. It's very important not to over-whip the cream or, if you're making it on a hot day, to allow it to become too warm, otherwise it will split when you fold it into the chocolate. Gradually fold the cream into the cooled white chocolate.

6 Pour the white chocolate mix onto the biscuit base and place in the fridge for an hour or so until it is firm.

7 To make the sauce, melt the dark chocolate over a pan of simmering water as you did the white chocolate. Add the double cream and stir together until smooth and glossy. Leave to cool until slightly stiff.

8 Decorate the top of the cake and leave to set or then serve the remaining sauce with the cake.

WHY NOT TRY...

Heating the knife in hot water before slicing the cake.

White chocolate-coated strawberry ice-cream balls

A quick, easy and impressive after-dinner treat or just a yummy indulgence.

250g/9oz good-quality
    strawberry ice cream
250g/9oz good-quality white
    chocolate, broken into
    pieces

Makes 16 balls
Prep time: 10 minutes plus
freezing

1 Place a plate in the freezer for about 30 minutes, then remove and cover with a sheet of baking parchment.

2 Using a melon baller, scoop the strawberry ice cream into balls. Remove from the baller with a wooden cocktail stick by pushing it into the ball. Place the ice-cream balls on the baking parchment, then return to the freezer for several hours or overnight, until frozen hard.

3 Put the chocolate into a heatproof bowl set over a pan of simmering water, making sure the water doesn't touch the base of the bowl. Leave until melted, stirring occasionally. Remove the bowl from the pan and leave for about 10 minutes, until the chocolate is no longer warm to the touch but is still liquid.

4 Dip the ice-cream balls into the white chocolate, slowly turning to ensure they are completely covered. Place them on the baking paper and return to the freezer. Freeze for at least 2 hours before serving. The white chocolate should be really hard and crack as you bite into it!

5 Allow to soften very, very slightly before serving.

WHY NOT TRY...

Great with mint ice cream and dark chocolate too – make in exactly the same way.

Chocolate soufflé cake with cherries and mascarpone

Ideally, make this pudding a day in advance but remember to take the cake out of the fridge 10 minutes before serving. Warm the compote through before serving and serve with fridge-cold mascarpone.

250g/9oz unsalted butter plus extra for greasing
250g/9oz dark chocolate (70% cocoa solids), broken into pieces
8 eggs, separated
250g/9oz caster sugar
chilled mascarpone cheese, to serve

FOR THE CHERRY COMPOTE
200g/7oz dried cherries
100ml/3¹/₂fl oz crème de Cassis
200ml/7fl oz water
1 star anise

Serves: 8
Prep time: 25 minutes
Cooking time: 30–35 minutes

1 Preheat the oven to 180°C/350°F/GM4. Grease a 23cm/9 inch springform cake tin with a little butter and line the base with baking parchment.

2 Put the butter and chocolate into a heatproof bowl set over a pan of simmering water, making sure the water doesn't touch the base of the bowl. Leave until melted, stirring occasionally.

3 In a large mixing bowl, whisk together the egg yolks and sugar with an electric mixer until pale and thick.

4 Wash the whisk well and, in the second mixing bowl, whisk the egg whites until they are stiff.

5 Pour the melted chocolate and butter into the egg yolk mixture and mix well.

6 Taking a large metal spoon, fold one quarter of the egg white into the chocolate, trying not to burst too many bubbles. Repeat the process a quarter at a time until all the egg white is mixed into the chocolate. Carefully pour the mixture into the cake tin. Bake in the oven for 30 minutes without opening the oven door. The surface of the cake will be cracked, but what you are looking for is the middle of the cake to wobble when you gently shake the tin, but it should also have started to set. If you think the cake is too sloppy, pop back in the oven for a further 5 minutes. It should be ready after that, but in case it's not, just repeat the process for another 5 minutes. When the cooking time is up, turn the oven off, open the oven door and leave

the tin in the oven until you are able to remove it
without using oven gloves. Leave to cool completely,
then place in the fridge to cool throughout.

7 Meanwhile, put all the cherry compote ingredients into
   a saucepan. Bring to the boil and simmer uncovered
   for 20 minutes. Remove from the heat, pop the lid on
   and leave for at least 30 minutes, or for as long as you
   want, depending upon how far in advance you are
   making it. Before you serve the compote, warm it
   through and remove the star anise.

8 Remove the cake from the fridge 10 minutes before
   serving. Heat the knife in a jug of hot water before
   slicing the cake and clean the knife each time with
   kitchen paper – this will give you cleanly cut pieces
   of cake. Serve each slice with a spoonful of warm
   compote and a dollop of cold mascarpone.

WHY NOT TRY...

**Use fresh cherries when
they're in season.**

Chocolate bread and butter pudding

Prepare this a day in advance and leave in the fridge until ready to cook. Serve with crème fraîche or vanilla ice cream to cut through the richness.

75g/3oz unsalted butter plus extra for greasing

1 × 300g brioche loaf, cut into about 10 slices

50g/2oz toasted hazelnuts, roughly chopped

300ml/10fl oz whipping cream

150g/5oz dark chocolate (70% cocoa solids), broken into pieces

1 tbsp golden syrup

4 eggs

crème fraîche or vanilla ice cream, to serve

Serves: 6–8
Prep time: 20 minutes
Cooking time: 30 minutes

1 Lightly grease a 20.5 × 25.5cm/8 × 10 inch baking dish. Cut each slice of brioche in half diagonally and arrange in the baking dish so that all the slices overlap slightly. You will probably have to do two layers of bread. Sprinkle the hazelnuts throughout the bread slices.

2 Put the butter, cream, chocolate and golden syrup into a heatproof bowl set over a pan of simmering water, making sure the water doesn't touch the base of the bowl, and simmer gently until the chocolate and butter have melted into the cream. Stir well.

3 In another mixing bowl, beat the eggs. Pour the melted chocolate mixture into the eggs and beat well until the sauce is smooth. Pour over the bread and leave for as long as possible. Ideally, make this pudding in the morning if it is needed for a dinner, or the night before if needed for a lunch.

4 When ready to cook, preheat the oven to 180°C/350°F/GM4. Bake the pudding for 30 minutes. Remove from the oven and allow to stand for about 10 minutes. Serve with crème fraîche or vanilla ice cream.

WHY NOT TRY...

For an extra chocolate hit, serve with a generous helping of the chocolate sauce on page 266.

Chocolate pancakes

The great thing about these is that they can be made very quickly and all the ingredients are storecupboard staples. Therefore, they make the perfect emergency pudding when you've forgotten a whole load of children are coming over for tea.

300ml/10fl oz semi-skimmed milk
100g/3^1/$_2$oz plain flour
20g/^{3}/$_4$oz good-quality cocoa powder
30g/1^1/$_4$oz caster sugar
^{1}/$_2$ tsp cinnamon powder
2 large eggs
^{1}/$_2$ tsp vanilla extract
30g/1^1/$_4$oz unsalted butter, melted, plus extra for frying
vanilla ice cream and maple syrup, to serve

Makes: 10 pancakes
Prep time: 10 minutes
Cooking time: 3 minutes per pancake

1 Simply place all the ingredients in a liquidizer and blitz for about 2 minutes. Alternatively, put all the dry ingredients into a large mixing bowl. Make a well in the middle and crack in the eggs. Beat in the eggs before gradually pouring in the milk, beating all the time, then add the vanilla extract and butter.

2 Pour the batter into a jug that is easy to pour from and leave for at least 30 minutes.

3 When you are ready to start cooking, warm a 23cm/ 9 inch non-stick frying pan or crêpe pan on a medium high heat. The first pancake is always a bit tricky, so melt 1 teaspoon of butter in the pan. When the butter is sizzling, add enough batter to evenly cover the bottom of the pan in a thin layer - tilt the pan quickly as you pour, so that the batter spreads out. Cook for 1–2 minutes until the pancake comes away easily from the edges of the pan when lifted with a spatula. If you feel brave, toss the pancake, although I think, after many failed attempts, it's probably easier to flip with a spatula. Cook for a further minute before turning out onto a waiting plate. Repeat to make 10 pancakes, regreasing the pan as necessary.

4 Fold each pancake in half. Top with a generous scoop of vanilla ice cream and drizzle with maple syrup.

WHY NOT TRY...

If you want even more chocolate in this chocolate heaven experience, drizzle some chocolate sauce (see page 266) on top.

All-purpose chocolate sauce

A very useful thing to have in your cooking repertoire is a good, easy chocolate sauce. Many's the time I've suddenly realized I have a load of children coming around for tea and I have nothing other than an old tub of vanilla ice cream nestling at the bottom of the freezer. Cooking chocolate, butter and golden syrup are storecupboard staples, and cream can be picked up at any garage on the way home. Add marshmallows, chopped nuts or hundreds and thousands and suddenly you have a pudding from heaven for most children (and many adults too!).

200g/7oz dark chocolate (70% cocoa solids), broken into pieces
150ml/5fl oz whipping cream (or double cream if no whipping cream available)
1 tbsp golden syrup
25g/1oz unsalted butter

Makes: 150ml/5fl oz
Prep time: 2 minutes
Cooking time: about 10 minutes

1 Find a saucepan and a heatproof bowl that fits snugly over the top. Put at least 3cm/1¼ inches of water in the bottom of the saucepan but make sure it doesn't touch the bottom of the bowl. Bring the water to the boil and reduce the heat immediately so that it barely simmers.

2 Place all the ingredients in the bowl and put on top of the saucepan. Allow the butter and the chocolate to melt and then whisk until the sauce is smooth and shiny.

3 Serve piping hot poured over ice cream, or anything else that needs perking up with a bit of chocolate!

WHY NOT TRY...

For sheer indulgence, serve with a bowl of the chocolate Malteser ice cream on page 268.

In our house, birthdays are real celebrations and whether it's a family affair with grandparents, aunts, uncles and cousins, or a party for the kids' friends, it can be pretty hectic once everyone's arrived. So if I'm going to have any chance to enjoy the day, too, I like to keep things informal and easy, particularly the food. When you're expecting an invasion from lots of children you don't want to be preparing dainty, fiddly finger food that they will only shove in their mouths without noticing that it is in the shape of an animal or football before they rush away from the table back to the games anyway. So my attitude is to save myself the disappointment and keep it simple.

Although we like the children to eat well, we know that birthdays are special and that if we have guests then we're catering for everyone's tastes, not just our own. Everyone expects treats at a party, and it would be a bit mean if we didn't bend the rules and bring out the classic kiddie treats – just don't go overboard, or you'll send them into a sugar frenzy and have a party full of hyperactive children! From personal experience of doing many kids' parties over the years, my best advice would be to plan and prepare as much in advance as you can – and make a lot of lists.

Chocolate Malteser ice cream

My favourite ever, ever, ever!

4 egg yolks

3 tbsp barley malt extract
(available at health
food stores and some
supermarkets)

284ml carton of whipping
cream, made up to
400ml/14fl oz with milk

100g/3¹/₂oz dark chocolate
(70% cocoa solids), broken
into pieces

150g/5oz Maltesers

cornets, to serve

Makes: about 600ml/1 pint
Prep time: 30 minutes plus
freezing

1 In a good-sized mixing bowl, beat together the egg
yolks and malt extract.

2 Pour the cream/milk mix into a medium saucepan and
add the chocolate. Put the saucepan on a low heat and
slowly heat through, stirring all the time to help the
chocolate melt. Do not let it boil.

3 When the chocolate has melted into the cream, pour it
over the egg mixture, beating well with a hand whisk.

4 Rinse out the saucepan and then pour the chocolate
mixture back into the pan. Again, on a low heat, cook
the custard gently, stirring all the time with a wooden
spoon. It is essential you do not allow it to boil or it
will separate and be ruined. The best way of doing this
is just to take it very slowly. As soon as the custard is
thick enough to coat the back of the spoon, pour it into
a clean mixing bowl and allow to cool.

5 When the mixture is cool, stir in the Maltesers and
pour into an ice-cream maker.

6 Following your particular model's instructions, allow
enough time to freeze. Serve in cornets.

Chocolate caramel slices

A perfect tea-time or lunchbox treat.

**FOR THE CHOCOLATE
BISCUIT BASE**
160g/5^{1}/$_{2}$oz unsalted butter
75g/3oz golden caster sugar
210g/7^{1}/$_{2}$oz plain white flour
30g/1^{1}/$_{4}$oz cocoa powder
^{1}/$_{2}$ tsp baking powder

FOR THE TOPPING
100g/3^{1}/$_{2}$oz butter
4 tbsp golden syrup
397ml can of condensed milk
100g/3^{1}/$_{2}$oz dark chocolate

Makes: 24 squares
Prep time: 30 minutes
Cooking time: 15–20 minutes

1 Preheat the oven to 180°C/350°F/GM 4 and line a 20.5 × 25.5cm/8 × 10 inch baking tray with baking parchment.

2 Place all the ingredients for the base in a food processor and process until they clump together into a ball. Using the back of a dessertspoon, spread the mixture into the tin, pushing down well to form an even layer. Put the tin in the oven and bake for 15–20 minutes, until the base is just firm to the touch. Remove from the oven and leave to cool.

3 Put the butter, golden syrup and condensed milk in a medium, heavy-based saucepan and heat gently, stirring occasionally, until the butter has melted. Bring to the boil, then reduce the heat and simmer for 5 minutes, stirring all the time. The mixture will thicken and turn into a pale golden caramel. Pour the caramel over the shortbread base, spread it evenly and leave to cool and set.

4 Break up the chocolate and place it in a heatproof bowl set over a pan of gently simmering water, making sure the water does not touch the base of the bowl. Leave to melt, stirring occasionally, then pour it over the caramel and spread out in an even layer. Leave until the chocolate has set – you may need to put it in the fridge. Cut into squares to serve.

Thanks

Karen, you've been fantastic – always ready to part with your endless knowledge and tricks. Working with you has been amazing.

Alex, once again you have been totally amazing – at times really against the odds – but as always so professional. Thank you.

Jill, what can I say? It has been a blast – the discussions during the photo shoots are best left unrevealed ... You've done an incredible job, thank you. And also to the lovely Zak.

Kate, thank you for always keeping an eagle eye out for me and being ready with your many tricks.

Jacqui and Susanna, once again you have surpassed yourselves. I was so against a different style of book but you fought against me and I love it. So OK, you were right!

Gary at Moens', thank you for the most amazing produce and for letting us invade your beautiful shop.

Finally, Gordon, Megan, Jack, Holly and Tilly, thank you for endlessly eating my recipes as they were created and tested – I love you all. x

Index